STEP ON THE MAT

STEP ON THE MAT

LIFE LESSONS OF THE NINJA

NINJA NGUYEN

LIONCREST
PUBLISHING

STEP ON THE MAT

Life Lessons of the Ninja

ISBN   978-1-5445-1322-5 *Hardcover*
      978-1-5445-1321-8 *Paperback*
      978-1-5445-1320-1 *Ebook*

CONTENTS

INTRODUCTION

In the middle of a war, I learned to fight.

Of course, I didn't completely understand the war going on, and I certainly wasn't fighting in the war itself. I was a four-year-old in Vietnam, the country where I was born, and my father had put me in a martial arts class. Even though that was where I first learned to punch, kick, and meditate, I wasn't really there to learn to fight. My dad just needed a place to put a curious kid who was asking too many questions—questions that could get my family in trouble.

I was one of ten children, the youngest of five brothers. And those brothers kept disappearing. I would ask my parents where my brothers were, and that simple question was the exact question my parents didn't need me asking. I would later learn that, one by one, my parents were smuggling my brothers out of the country to keep them from having to fight in the war. In Vietnam at that time, once you hit eighteen, you went into the military. You had no choice—unless you escaped. My parents wanted my brothers to escape.

By smuggling my brothers out of Vietnam, my father was taking a great risk. If caught, he would be thrown in jail. One day, he would be caught. But in the meantime, he was busy fishing, getting my brothers out of the country, and trying to find a place for his little boy with too many questions.

That place was a martial arts class. And my father's decision to put me there would shape the rest of my life.

MY FIRST DOJO

The word "dojo" might bring a different picture to mind here. The first dojo of my childhood wasn't a building full of mats and trophies. It was in the backyard of a local man's home, under a large awning. We didn't have traditional uniforms, just the clothes we wore every day. There were no mats, just the hard, bare ground. We had no belts. In fact, it wasn't until years later that I knew what belts even were.

I still remember that first class, coming in with no experience and everyone being better than I was. I got in line with everyone else—and I was at the end of the line. Because there were no belt rankings, we lined up according to who had trained the longest or who worked the hardest in training and helped the instructor around the dojo.

Once we were lined up, we began our routine. We bowed to the instructor. We stood in a wide, deep squat called "horse stance," because it looks like you're sitting on an invisible horse, to work our leg muscles. After standing in horse stance we went through our basic punches and kicks. I didn't know what I was doing that first day, but as it turned out, I was learning a routine that would bring structure to my life from then on. During the next two years, I trained at the dojo every day.

I fell in love with training. I liked what I was learning. Not only the techniques, but also the discipline. I knew that if I wanted to be noticed, I had to be disciplined. I had to show up every day, do the stretching, and put in the work. I had to practice. I had to prove myself to my mentor and teacher.

Being a young kid with two parents working to raise us in the middle of a war, the dojo was also a place where I could feel at peace. It was the only place where I could express myself, even if it was through punches and kicks instead of words.

I continued to train every day, learning to punch the maki-wara—a board wrapped tightly in ropes—and standing in water to add resistance to kicks. It was hard work, but it was fun. I never wanted to stop. And then everything changed.

MOVING ON

My dad was arrested for smuggling out four of my brothers. He spent two years in jail, and when he was released, my family had no place to live. We fled the country.

I remember being on a boat and seeing an island. I thought it was America, but America was over nine thousand miles away. I was looking at Malaysia.

It was 1979. We stayed in a Malaysian camp for a year before we moved on to the Philippines, where we lived in another refugee camp. This was an interesting place, full of nice people all locked behind a gate. We weren't allowed to leave until someone sponsored us to come to the US. I could see people and cities beyond our camp, but it was all on the other side of a tall fence that kept us from ever going anywhere else.

It was in that camp that I found my second martial arts instructor. It wasn't in a dojo or even someone's house. It was in a kitchen. Every morning, everyone in the camp would get in line for food and as it turned out, the chef at the camp was a martial artist.

Every day I would get in line early to get food for my family. If you were late, there wasn't always much food left, so I wanted to make sure I was there in time. One day I tried to show off for the people giving out the food. I did some martial arts moves, punching and kicking with some of the other kids. I hadn't been in a martial arts class for years, but I'd never forgotten what I'd learned.

The chef saw me and stopped what he was doing. He came up to me and corrected my technique. Then he showed me some new moves. I had no idea what rank he was, or even what martial art he knew, but I didn't care. I had an instructor again, and martial arts was there for me once more. I visited the instructor every day with my friends, and when we came through the line, he would teach us a little something.

He came close to being the last instructor I would ever have.

A NEW WORLD

My family lived in the Philippine refugee camp for nearly two years before we finally made it to the US in December 1980. I was ten years old then, and everything in America was different from anything I'd ever experienced before. For one thing, it was freezing! I had never seen snow before and thought it was wonderful, even if it was cold. I was mesmerized by the snowflakes drifting through the air and how they would collect in soft piles. I had fun crunching the snow under my boot and making snow-balls. There was also music on the TV all the time. Back home, the closest thing to television I'd experienced was an outdoor movie played through a projector. A group came to our village about once a month and put one on. In America, I also couldn't believe how much candy there was in the convenience stores, how the stoplights seemed to turn everything outside red (there had been no stoplights at all in my village), or that the windows in our new home had glass in them, keeping the flies out.

All of that was great, but school was a different story. I didn't speak any English, and it was hard to adjust. Lucky for me, there was a teacher at the school who helped kids like me learn English. He was also Vietnamese and, like me, he was a martial artist. He told me I needed to find a dojo. Once again, martial arts had come into my life.

I already had a dojo in mind. I walked by it every day on my way to and from school, and I watched students through the windows. It had been a long time since my days learning to punch and kick in line at the refugee camp—longer since I'd been in that first dojo in my village, and I missed training. I needed a place where I could fit in and belong, and where I could express myself in the way I knew how.

Even with an English tutor, learning the language of my new country was hard. In class, I would try and be discouraged. Once, I raised my hand and tried to read aloud like the rest of the kids, but I could not make out the words. In the dojo, trying, even if it meant failing, was rewarded, but in my classroom this wasn't the case. Instead of encouraging or praising me for having the guts to try, my teacher simply said, "You're wrong." The way she said it was devastating. I never raised my hand again after that.

I badly wanted to join that dojo, but my dad didn't want me to. In Vietnam, martial arts had been a way to keep me busy, but in America, he had different plans for me. My job was to go to school and get an education so I could have a career and make money.

"Martial arts are not a business," my father would say.

I respected my father, and I obeyed him. But one day, I couldn't take it anymore. I walked into the dojo. I sat on a chair in the corner and watched the students. I returned again and again to that chair in the dojo, punching and kicking in my seat while I watched the students train. Finally, the instructor came over to me. "Do you like martial arts?" he asked—or at least I think that's what he asked. I couldn't understand his English. He motioned me over, saying, "Come, come." That much I understood. I got up and followed him. I stepped on the mat.

After that, I went to the dojo every day for two weeks. I would walk in, put my shoes away, clean the dojo as payment, and train.

The dojo was the place where I continued learning martial arts, but it was also the place where I found friends and fit in. It was also where I learned to speak English. The instructor would say, "Front punch." I didn't know the words, but I recognized the punch, and I began to associate the words. By learning karate (and watching plenty of *Mr. Rogers' Neighborhood*), I slowly began to learn English and found my place in a new country.

I loved my father. He taught me things about life that I still carry with me and have passed on to my own children. But he was completely wrong about martial arts. Not only were they a way to build a business, they became the foundation on which I built my life.

MY OWN DOJO

As soon as I graduated high school, I opened my first dojo. By that point, I was a skilled competitive fighter. But I had begun to lose my way as a martial artist. My dad must have noticed, because he said to me, "If you open a school, you need to make sure you are a teacher, not a student."

Well, this was one of the many times when dad was right.

I should have listened to him. The truth was, I didn't open the dojo to teach students as much as I opened it to keep training. I didn't see it as a place to teach; I saw it as a place to train. I didn't see the people who came to the dojo as students; I saw them as sparring partners. I would beat them whenever I could, and if I couldn't, I'd just hit harder. If I was teaching them anything, it was to be fighters, not martial artists.

Because I saw my students as sparring partners, I wasn't a very effective teacher. My dad told me, "Number one, you have to expect your students to become better than you, because that's your job as a teacher. Number two, don't forget that when you open a school, you become a teacher. Don't expect your students to say 'thank you' to you. That's not why you open a school."

Within a few years, I had to close the dojo. No one wanted me as their teacher.

With the dojo out of my life, I began to lose my way. I began working security in a nightclub in Boston. My job wasn't to check IDs. Rather, I was there to stop fights and kick out anyone who started trouble. Needless to say, it was not the best environment for me at a time when I was so focused on being a fighter.

I lived that life for eleven years and slowly became lost in the lifestyle that can come with working in a nightclub. I got to know drug dealers and gangsters. In time, I started selling drugs myself. I was the guy in the club who had access to all the customers. They would ask me where to get something, and I would tell them who to talk to. I started to make good money while my life fell apart.

During this time, I was still training in martial arts, but I was not living the life of a martial artist. Sometimes, I would teach at a friend's school. I would tell kids things like, "Stay away from drugs," and then I would go back to the nightclub and hang out with drug dealers. I was saying one thing and doing another. That's not the life of a martial artist.

I was unhappy. The only moments when I thought I was happy was when there was a fight in the club and I could get involved, putting my martial arts skills to use. Even then, however, my martial arts training—true martial arts training—would return to me, because when I kicked someone out, I realized I couldn't *just* be violent. I didn't want to hurt them, and I understood that I had to listen to them if I wanted them to listen to me. I genuinely wanted them to get home safe. I remembered to listen and be present.

But that wasn't enough to save me from myself.

Soon, I met my wife. Anna was a bartender in the same club where I worked. She was hardworking and beautiful. Before long we'd fallen in love and moved in together. We were supposed to be starting our life together, but I had a hard time leaving some of my old habits behind. I kept hanging around with the wrong people, doing the wrong things. We moved around a bit, eventually landing in Arizona. We thought a drastic change in scenery might be what we needed, but it didn't change anything. Anna was quickly tiring of my behavior.

When we had our first daughter, I knew I had to change.

We were in Arizona and I once again found myself managing a nightclub, back in my old habits. Lucky for me, the club's owner had my best interests at heart. Tom Cerino looked like he was straight out of one of *The Godfather* movies, but he didn't set me on the path of being a gangster. He started me on the path to saving myself. He must have seen something in me, because he recommended a self-improvement course. It helped. I learned more about myself, about relationships, about what was really important.

It helped, but not enough, and not quickly enough. Our marriage had already suffered so much damage, and I wasn't proving to Anna that I was making progress. We went bankrupt, and she left, telling me I would never really change.

"Yes I will," I told her. She left, and I set out to straighten out my life.

I went back home, and into the dojo.

SAVED IN THE DOJO

I returned home to Boston and while I was trying to figure things out, I began teaching for a former student of mine,

Pat Matthews, who owned a dojo. I was teaching for free simply because I loved it and because it felt so good to be back where I had always felt most at home. When the owner of the dojo asked me to help him open a new school near Cape Cod, I told him of course I would, and I did.

Once his new dojo was open, he handed me a set of keys. These were to his other dojo—the one where'd I'd been helping him teach. It was mine now, he said, if I wanted it. I didn't have to pay a dime. As long as I could take over the cost of rent, the dojo was mine.

I knew this was my chance to make everything right. At the time, there were about ten students in the dojo. I worked as hard as I could to build it up. Today, I have 560 students.

My wife saw me turning my life around and returned with our daughter, who we'd named Patience. (I'd wanted to name her that because I knew good things didn't happen all at once—that they required patience.) Shortly after this, my second daughter was born. Life was so good then, so full of love, that I could only think of one name for her: Harmony.

Not long after Harmony was born, my parents passed away. One of the last things my dad said to me before he died was, "I'm proud of you. You're the man I know you're meant to be."

My dad's name was Cao, which means "high," in Vietnamese. When my son was born, I named him Sky, for my dad.

LIFE AS A MARTIAL ARTIST

Today, I still own and run my Boston dojo. I am still married and raising my three amazing children. You could say that I am a successful businessman because that's true. But what I really am is a successful martial artist. It was martial arts and the lessons they taught me that have allowed me to have the life I have today.

My successes today, like the failures I experienced, were the consequences of my choices. The choices that have led to success and love and joy in my life are the consequences of the lessons I now want to share with you in this book.

In a sense, this book is a journey through what I have learned during my life. But it is also a journey through one of my martial arts classes. Everything contained in the following pages can be found in just one class. In fact, this book will essentially lead you step-by-step through one of my classes and show you the lessons you can learn between the moment you enter the dojo and step on the mat, and the moment you step off the mat and back into your life.

So join me. Let's head to the dojo. Let's step on the mat.

CHAPTER 1

✳ ❄ ✳

BOW

LESSON: COMMITMENT
RULE: ACKNOWLEDGMENT
GOAL: STAY COMMITTED

In our everyday lives, we're often unaware of our own movements. When we stand up from sitting or lying down, we're not conscious of where we put our feet or our weight. When we walk around, we don't think about our balance—about the motion and momentum in our bodies.

In martial arts, we are aware of these movements. We acknowledge how we move, who we move with, who we learn from, and how we make our way in the world. We acknowledge our respect and our commitment. As martial artists, we acknowledge everything, and are aware of everything. We're aware of ourselves.

We practice that acknowledgment and awareness with the bow.

In martial arts, you will learn all kinds of skills that can enable you to defend yourself or lead you to victory in competition. But those skills and lessons can also transcend the dojo and apply to your everyday life.

And the first skill is the bow.

WHAT BOWING TEACHES US

Why can't more of us use this practice in the outside world? How each moment unfolds in your life depends on your attitude, your commitment to what you believe in, and your awareness of your situation. By bowing, we remind ourselves that we aren't martial artists only in the dojo, but everywhere and at every moment.

ACKNOWLEDGMENT

A bow in martial arts is the same as a handshake in America. It's a way of offering respect and acknowledgment.

Acknowledgment is important. We often forget this and take the important things in life for granted. Or we do things we know we're supposed to do, but we fail to really acknowledge them; we just go through the motions.

Worse yet, sometimes we find excuses for our problems instead of solutions to them.

When we bow, we take the time to acknowledge the important things in life—our responsibilities, our commitments, and the people we care about.

You bow to your partner to acknowledge them and give them respect. You bow to the dojo to acknowledge your training. Inwardly, you may bow to your girlfriend or boyfriend before you take them on a date to acknowledge the importance of the moment and that your date deserves your respect. You bow before you step on the mat to acknowledge that you are there to *train*, not to simply go through the motions.

When we practice bowing, we practice acknowledgment and offering respect.

COMMITMENT

When you bow, you make a commitment. It's not just a movement, it's the way you signal to yourself that you are committed to the moment.

Let's say, for example, that a student of mine has just been dumped by his girlfriend. He's depressed, and he keeps thinking of her and how sad he is about what happened. Then he enters the dojo, and the first thing he does is bow. He is expressing his commitment. He's expressing it to the dojo itself, to the training partners he has there, to his sensei—but he is also expressing to himself that he is here to train. Everything bothering him is going to have to wait a while, because he has learned to commit himself to his training. He has learned the true meaning of the bow.

Committing to Choices

Imagine I'm driving along the highway and see a sign telling me my lane is about to end. Then I see another car in the other lane, coming up behind me. As a driver, I have a choice to make. I can slow down to let that car go ahead of me, or I can move over into another lane myself first.

Now imagine I let the other car go in front of me. I realize that this person is an incredibly slow driver. My instinct may be to complain. But if I truly understand commitment, I know that complaining isn't really an option. I chose to let that driver go ahead of me. I can't expect that car to go at my speed just because I gave way.

Life is all about choices. In every situation, you choose in or out. If you choose in, you have to accept the consequences of the decision you've made.

The same dynamic applies in a martial arts gym. Imagine I'm training with someone new. They become my partner. Because they're new, they don't know as many concepts or details as I do. It's my responsibility to know what they're capable of. In that scenario, I have to ask myself if I want that person to train better or not. Maybe I wish I had a better partner because I'd wanted a different kind of sparring session. But what I wanted a few minutes ago no longer matters, because I've made my choice.

In life, we spar all the time—at school, on the road driving. We make our choices and we must stand by them. We don't always get to spar the way we want, but we have to commit to the choices we have made and deal with the consequences of them. Sometimes that means we have to be polite when it's tough or support others when we're more interested in ourselves. But if the situation we've chosen calls for politeness or supporting others, we have to honor that.

Always ask yourself: do you want to be a better person? If you do, you need to inspire and be helpful to other people. Discouraging others only creates more hate in both of your lives. It does no good to honk at a slow driver just as it does no good to spar too hard with a beginner. Nobody needs more hate.

When a student comes into my gym, I say, "don't forget what you bow yourself into."

I always remind them because I never want them to forget about the commitment they're making. One of the first lessons I teach students is how to have their feet together in what we call the attention stance. With their next movement, they bow, and go into the defense stance, with one foot forward and one foot backward, similar to the warrior pose in yoga.

I never want students to forget the commitments they make. When my students go into the commitment stance, I ask them what the word dojo means. As soon as they define dojo, I ask them to give me their word that they will take their training seriously. If they say they're going to train, I want them to commit to training.

HOW TO BOW

The bow might seem like a simple movement, but it's more complicated than it sounds. In fact, there are different ways of bowing. The first bow I learned in martial arts—the karate bow—is different than the bow of kung fu, for example.

The way you bow also depends on who is standing in

front of you. If they're a training partner, for example, you would maintain eye contact with them while you bowed. But if the person is someone for whom you have a greater level of respect—say, your teacher or a master—you would bow without making eye contact.

Below, I'll explain how I teach students to bow. But don't worry if you sign up at a dojo and they teach a different way. The idea and meaning of the bow remain constant. There are simply different ways to do it, depending on style.

The karate bow begins in attention stance, with your feet together, and your hands by your sides. Beginning with your body straight, bend forward at the waist. As you bend over, keep your hands by your sides, your fingers pointing down. You are tilting into what we call the "sun bow."

I learned how to bow as a child in Vietnam. I was taught that when a person surrenders, their hands are not in front of them to block or push another person away—and that is what we symbolize when we bow with our hands at our sides. We are showing the other person that we mean no harm and that we respect them. In a way, we are surrendering. When we surrender, we acknowledge the other person. There is no more resistance to yourself or the other person. I incorporate these same lessons into my teaching today.

The first thing a martial artist does upon entering a dojo is bow. When you do this, not everyone will notice, but that doesn't matter, because the bow is for you. It is to remind yourself that you are now training. You are acknowledging your commitment to the practice, to the art, and to your fellow martial artists.

You're also bowing to the dojo itself. The word dojo means "the place where you learn the way." (In martial arts, the word "do" translates to "the way.") Sometimes I ask my students what the difference is between a dojo and a playground, and at this point they all know the answer: a playground is a place to play, whereas a dojo is a place to learn. It's still a place for fun, but it's also a place of serious commitment toward bettering yourself.

The dojo is a sacred place, and the bow is a sacred act. A martial artist bows not only when entering the dojo, but also when he or she steps onto the mat to begin training. The bow is a student's sign of respect, acknowledgment, and commitment to the training space and to his or her partners. Students bow to their instructors and their training partners before and after sparring. They also bow off the mat and, finally, they bow out of the dojo.

That sounds like a lot of bowing, and maybe it is. But a lot of bowing leads to an increased awareness of what you're doing and what you're committed to. And bowing doesn't have to stop in the dojo. The bow is the first thing you can take with you when you leave the dojo. Many martial artists bow in front of almost everything they do. They bow before work, before they come home, and in front of their girlfriends to acknowledge them.

TIPS ON BOWING

Once you have a feel for what the bow means, your understanding of it can grow. Here are some more thoughts on what the bow means in the dojo and in your life.

ACKNOWLEDGE THE MOMENT

How often does it happen that a kid asks their parents for a toy and, after the parents buy that toy, the kid plays with it for only a few days (or even a few moments) and soon enough, forgets all about it? How often do we capture our accomplishments, victories, and happy moments by snapping a picture on our phone and putting it on social media before forgetting all about it? How often are we truly aware of what we've done or what we're doing in the moment?

Every single day—every single moment—is an opportunity to get better. But often, people do not treat them this way. Fridays are celebrated in America. I always hear people say, "TGIF!" The final bell rings at school, and all the students run for the door to escape. Working people get their paycheck and spend it on their weekend.

But why can't we celebrate every moment of our lives? Why do we wait until our birthdays to celebrate ourselves? We should be able to celebrate everything we do, every day.

This is why we bow. It's why we bow so much. We're committed to the moment. We acknowledge the small, but important times and opportunities of our lives.

Every time I wake up in the morning, I'm happy. I'm grateful for the fact that my eyes have opened and that I'm breathing. As a parent, I feel overwhelmed with gratitude when I see my healthy children breathing next to me. However, most of the time, people forget to feel grateful for these moments.

As martial artists, we learn to treasure these moments through our awareness and our acknowledgment. We treasure our moments.

It's not always easy. I'm a teacher, and I sometimes work with kids that have a hard time listening. But I know I can't give up on students like that. You can't call yourself a teacher if you give up on the kids who need you the most. I know to treasure the moments I can spend teaching them, and I hope that my students learn to treasure the moments when they're being taught. I can't give up on them, and I don't want them to give up on me.

In the modern age, it's easy to forget to treasure the moments we share with each other. We're so distracted, we forget to talk to each other. Everybody has a phone or a tablet in their hands. When kids hang out with their parents, even the parents are on the phone! My kids are four, six, and ten years old. In my house, we have a no-phone rule. Every time our family goes somewhere together, my kids say, "Daddy, no phone."

And that's that. We hang out, no phone. We go to the beach, no phone. We go to a restaurant, no phone. I'm with my kids. Who do I need to talk to?

In my life, I always try to treasure the things around me. I want my kids and my students in the dojo to do the same thing. How can I expect my kids to be better than I if I'm not setting a good example? You can't expect someone to love you if you don't love yourself. You can't want someone to take care of you if you can't take care of yourself. When you learn to treasure each moment, you'll be teaching others how to do the same thing just by setting the example.

All those moments we commit to and acknowledge add up.

Staying committed means you're in it for the long haul. It means you're ready for the ups and downs, the disappointments and failures. When you stay committed, it means you're acknowledging that this is not about singular moments or accomplishments. It means you recognize that you are on a lifelong journey.

As martial artists, we recognize how hard we work to deserve our ranks in the dojo. Our ranks reflect our accomplishments. They're benchmarks that remind us of where we are along our journey.

In relationships and life, people might recognize other kinds of benchmarks—birthdays, anniversaries—and celebrate them for a brief moment. But when the moment ends, so does the appreciation. As martial artists, however, through the practice of commitment and acknowledgment, we see benchmarks for what they are. Like the belts we wear in the dojo, we take these moments with us, continually aware of where we are on our journeys.

Don't forget the goal. Don't forget the lesson. Don't forget the rule.

Commit. Acknowledge. Stay committed.

In life, everyone has had an experience of playing the victim.

Picture this. I have entered a jiu-jitsu tournament. It is my turn to fight. I step onto the mat and bow to my opponent. We begin, and he submits me.

I have two choices. I can respect that my opponent has bested me, learn from my mistakes, and get back to work, or I can get upset and make excuses for why I lost. In other words, I can play the victim. Victims are people who never think they are at fault. They are people who can't take responsibility.

That's why I must tap out. (This is really another form of bowing.) I must acknowledge I have been beaten and congratulate my partner. By bowing in the first place, I chose my way into this situation, and now I must be prepared for all consequences.

It's the same with the example of the slow driver. You can't blame the other driver for the consequences of your actions. You let the other car cut in, and now the driver is allowed to move slowly. If you want to move faster, you either have to find another route or find a way to move past the driver. Regardless of what you do, the situation is your fault. It was your choice.

The bottom line is this: If you choose to stay the same, you can't play the victim. You can't blame others for the consequences of your choices.

A BOWING STORY

When I came to the US in the 1980s, the culture was different from the way it is today. It seemed as though everyone had a mutual interest in being part of a safe and loving community. My mother never locked our front door. We could run around the neighborhood and all feel safe. I wasn't that into baseball when I played, but I remember the field as a peaceful place with no one yelling at each other.

Somewhere along the line, things changed. Now everyone, it seems, has to lock their door. Parents are afraid to let their kids run around their own neighborhoods. You go to a baseball game nowadays, and you'll see parents screaming at each other.

The one place I know of where this hasn't changed in America is the dojo. Sure, there might be some bad martial arts gyms out there, but overall, dojos remain a place of peace and respect.

And much of that has to do with the bow.

In my gym now, I'm reminded of how things were when I grew up. I've created an environment of peace and mutual respect. Even when we go to a tournament—a place where we go to fight each other!—I'm always pleased to see the other martial artists I know from other gyms. We shake hands, we bow, we talk, and laugh. The bow reminds us how to live in peace.

BEYOND THE DOJO

When we began this chapter, it's likely that you never gave bowing much thought. Maybe you saw it in movies or even in a martial arts class. But bowing is important.

Everything begins with the bow.

Everything begins with the choice to commit, acknowledge, and stay committed.

When you go to school, bow. When you go out with your friends, bow. When you help your parents around the house, bow. When you get in your car, bow.

Even if you're only bowing in your own head, bow. Make the commitment. Stand by your choices. Live as a true martial artist.

FOR THE PARENTS

Most parents who don't do martial arts don't understand what a bow is or what it represents.

Think about it this way. As a parent, you're constantly making choices and commitments. You make a commitment to pick up your kid from class, for example. When you choose to pick your kid up, you're not just committing to playing taxi driver. You're bowing into the whole process. You have to be willing to ask them about their day. When you ask about their day, you have to be willing to care and listen. I see so many parents who ask their kids questions and then don't listen to the answer. "I'm busy," they say. "Here's the tablet."

If my kids come to hang out with me, but then start doing other things, I ask them what they actually want. Usually, their answer is that they want to hang out with me. When you choose to become a parent, you choose to spend time with your kids.

As a parent, you should learn the lesson of the bow. You've already chosen into the parent role. It's your job to commit, acknowledge, and stay committed to that choice in each interaction. Practice the bow. Take the moment to remember what you've chosen into, and commit to it. Choose *in*.

Perhaps your child has a martial arts instructor. Perhaps they've been taught what bowing is. But their biggest influence is you. You're the one who will show them what bowing—commitment, acknowledgment, and staying committed—*really* means, because you should be that committed to them.

CHAPTER 2

✳ ✳ ✳

MEDITATE

LESSON: FOCUS AND SELF-REFLECTION
RULE: BREATHE
GOAL: FIND BALANCE

The second thing we do in my martial arts classes, once we have bowed in, is meditate.

Now that we've made the commitment, it's time to access our best selves before we begin practicing any technique.

Meditation offers us a chance to find focus and self-reflection, to practice and remember the importance of breathing, and to find inner balance—all things that are essential for a true martial artist.

WHAT MEDITATION TEACHES US

It's easy to get caught up in the idea that we should expect something from meditation. Meditation does have lots of benefits. But the tricky thing about it is that when you get caught up in thinking about those benefits—if you're waiting for them to happen to you or trying to make them happen—you can defeat the whole purpose.

The best thing to do is just, well, meditate. Over time, you will notice the benefits. You just can't force them to happen.

Again, just breathe.

FOCUS AND SELF-REFLECTION

Focusing can be hard, and it's harder for some of us than for others. Meditation is, in a sense, just practicing the art of being focused. When we're sparring, playing a video game, or doing some other fun activity, it's easier to be focused and engaged. But when all we're focusing on is our breathing, it's tougher. It can seem boring at first! But as you get better at it, you learn what it is to be truly focused. You also get to know yourself a bit better as you acknowledge all those thoughts passing through your head. (More on this in just a moment.)

When my students learn to control their breathing, they

learn to be more calm. It's important to feel calm before you train. Just as you don't want to be lost in distracting thoughts during meditation, you certainly don't want to be lost in thoughts when you train. If you're lost in thought, how can you focus on improving your technique? How can you be truly listening to your teacher? Imagine sparring with a skilled opponent and being lost in thought—that could be dangerous!

When you learn how to focus on your breathing, you experience being in the moment. And when you're training—and especially when you're fighting—you must be in the present moment.

You must also remain focused on goals. In my class, I give students a goal every day. When they bow onto the mat, they are acknowledging that goal. When they meditate, they are focusing their minds on that goal. When we begin to train, they take that goal with them.

BREATHE

The first step in meditation is to simply breathe. Get into a comfortable position, close your eyes, and feel your body breathe. Listen to the breath. Pay attention to it.

To meditate, you don't have to close your eyes. It's enough to sit still and focus on your breathing. Or you can engage in walking meditation. If you choose this option, simply walk slow, listen to your breath, and take time to notice the things around you and be present with them.

Breathing is the rule because, well, that's all there really is to do. When in doubt, lost in thought, or doing anything else other than breathing, remember the rule. Go back to the breath.

There's no right or wrong way to breathe. There shouldn't be anything to fight or overthink. While you're meditating, all you need to do is focus on your breath.

Just breathe.

FIND BALANCE

Physical balance is one thing, but what about mental and spiritual balance? This is the ultimate goal of meditation. At first, it can be hard to even know what this is. If you've never meditated, you may not even know how out of balance you are!

That's okay. Meditation, like martial arts, is something we practice over the course of our lives. I'm still seeking balance myself, and I've been doing this my whole life!

Meditation helps us recognize when we're out of balance—

when our emotions or negative thoughts are overtaking our minds. Often, when we're having negative thoughts or feelings, we never take the time to really notice. We just act on them without thinking. Meditation helps us take a step back, notice these things about ourselves, and act deliberately.

In other words, it offers us balance.

HOW TO MEDITATE

These days, everyone talks about meditation and alignment. However, I'm not sure how many people understand the true benefit of meditation—or even what it is.

When I lead meditation, I tell my students that the most important thing is to focus on their breathing. Breathe in and breathe out.

That's it.

Or at least, that's supposed to be it. Meditation really is as simple as just breathing—but simple doesn't mean easy.

TIPS ON MEDITATION

So, just breathe. No problem, right? Well, there's a reason

I said it's not easy. Just paying attention to your breathing can, as I've said, feel pretty boring at first. And when the brain gets bored, it starts to wander. Meditation is about breathing, but it's also about *returning to breathing*. It's about getting to know yourself, seeing when you're distracted, catching yourself, and getting back to what you're supposed to be doing—breathing.

Here are some tips to help you.

DON'T FIGHT YOUR THOUGHTS

Go ahead and try not to think for the next minute or so. Go ahead. I'll wait.

Well, how did it go? Did you have a thought? One you didn't expect? Welcome to meditation—the place where we discover just how many thoughts we have rattling around in our brains even when, or especially when, we don't want to.

People often say that meditation is about clearing your mind, but that's a misconception. How could you ever truly clear your mind? Go ahead and try. See how long it takes before thoughts start to pop up.

In meditation, you shouldn't fight your thoughts. (It's supposed to be a calming exercise—you shouldn't be fighting anything!) Instead, you should simply acknowledge them as they come. Don't spend time on your thoughts. Don't get lost in them. Just acknowledge them as normal occurrences and let each one drift on by as you return your attention to your breath.

When another thought drifts in, simply acknowledge it as well, and then let it go on its way as you once again return your attention to your breathing.

Do this over and over.

That's meditation.

FOCUS

There are a few ways to focus during meditation.

First, feel your breath. Feel it where you inhale and exhale. Feel your body move with the breath. Explore it. Get to know your breath.

Second, feel each pulse in your body. Pay attention to every heartbeat. Paying attention is key. You can really only focus on one thing at a time. The better you become at focusing on your breathing, the less often thoughts will interrupt you.

Don't worry if it's difficult at first. While some people

have no problem meditating, others struggle with fighting their thoughts. Some people can't sit still. There's nothing wrong with that. Remember, this will take time and practice.

Just breathe.

FIND A RHYTHM

Meditation should be practiced regularly. Like anything else, with regular practice comes improvement and benefits.

Dedicate a few of minutes each day to meditation. That's all it takes. Start small if you need to, and build from there. If you do this consistently, you'll discover a rhythm of breathing that works for you.

Meditation provides a routine for my students. They know that when they walk into the dojo, they bow and start meditating. This teaches them to be more focused. They acknowledge their thoughts without fighting them. When they're done with meditation, their minds are focused, and they are ready to train.

You can do this in your daily life as well as on the mats. What is the best time for you to meditate every day?

During mediation in my gym, I encourage my students to breathe in positive energy and breathe out negative energy. That's the rhythm I teach. Once you get used to that rhythm, you can control your breathing. Then, you can test yourself to make your inhalations and exhalations longer.

With every breath, I tell my students to focus on their abdominal area. In America they call this the "core." In martial arts we call it "chi."

Some kids struggle to understand the concept of chi. If you're struggling, think about the times when you get upset. Where do you get that energy from? How do you make a strong noise? When people think in those terms, they find it easier to tune into that energy—into chi.

The flow of energy is important in training. Imagine someone who doesn't practice breathing or meditation regularly. When somebody punches them, they're going to get hurt.

Now imagine someone who *does* practice breathing and meditation regularly. When someone punches them, their body seals up to protect itself. That person has an energy flow. You need to create a flow of energy to avoid getting hurt when you train.

To create an energy flow, breathe in and out. Put your hand in front of you. Inhale, exhale. At first, you might not feel any hot air. However, once you do this about ten times, you'll see the energy flowing. Heat starts coming up. This is an energy inside your body which is flowing out. That's chi.

You can create your chi through certain movements. For example, tai chi focuses only on breathing, but karate is more focused on hard hits. In my gym, we encourage students to meditate and work on breathing to better their chi. If you want a stronger energy flow, you don't have to hit things. You have to practice your breathing. You have to create connection by inhaling and exhaling.

You won't wake up one day and suddenly know how to create chi. It's an ongoing lesson. I'm still learning it myself.

BE PRESENT WITH YOURSELF AND OTHERS

Every time you bow into training, ask yourself: am I being present? Every time you learn a lesson, acknowledge what you're learning. Acknowledge your skin. Acknowledge your body. Acknowledge your breath. Finally, identify your focus for each lesson. Repeat this process for every training session, every lesson.

Meditation is an intense practice of being present in

the moment, acknowledging and moving beyond your thoughts and feelings as you feel your inhalations and exhalations.

During meditation, practice that feeling of presence so that you might take it with you elsewhere.

LEARN TO ENJOY YOU

Your time spent meditating is time spent with yourself. Not everyone likes themselves. Meditation provides an opportunity to get to know yourself and learn to like yourself—or to like yourself more. After all, if you can't stand to spend time with yourself, how can you expect anyone else to want to? Learn how.

A MEDITATION STORY

After my daughter was born, I lost my business. I wasn't immediately sure what to do, but I did know what I needed to do: take care of my family.

Every day, I woke up knowing only that I must feed my child and be the best father I could be.

I had two options. The first was that I could listen to the voice in my head, telling me that I couldn't do it, that I didn't deserve to be a father and succeed as one. It wasn't only my voice saying it. At this point in my life my wife also wasn't sure if I could succeed, and told me that if I didn't, I would never see my baby.

But there was another voice, the one I chose to focus on. This voice said, "I have to."

My mind went back and forth between these two voices, and it was through meditation that I was able to properly focus on the right one. Every night before I went to bed I would see that my baby had food and clothes, and I would meditate, focusing on making sure she continued to be taken care of.

I owe much of my success to my ability to meditate—to focus on the right things and not be distracted by the wrong things.

Because I was able to maintain my focus I was able not only to build the business I have today, but to accomplish my ultimate goal to be a good husband and father.

BEYOND THE DOJO

I've talked a lot about meditating before training, but you may have noticed that I mentioned a lot of times outside the dojo when you should be meditating—like every day!

That's because like everything we learn in martial arts, meditation isn't something that just exists in the dojo. You train in the dojo to become a better person—a true martial artist, not just a fighter.

Being focused in your training doesn't just apply to fighting. When you're at school, you're training. When you're eating or with your family—or anywhere—you should be present. You should always be focused on the moment.

For example, when I go to church, I know I have two choices. Either I can focus and be present or I can let myself get distracted and spend the entire time watching other people fool around or simply get lost in my own thoughts. When I walk into church, I identify my goal for that day.

Personally, I go to church to pray. That's my goal. I acknowledge what I want to get out of every church experience. Throughout my time sitting in the pew, I often have to remind myself of my goal. For example, if I catch someone fooling around near me, I remind myself to focus on breathing. When I control my breathing, I go back to my focus. I remember my goal.

Guess what? That's meditation. I got distracted, acknowledged it, and brought myself back to the present moment. In formal meditation, we do it with our breathing. In real life, we bring ourselves back to our goal, whether that's our homework, paying attention in church, or having a conversation with a friend.

In life, it's normal to lose track of your goals sometimes. There's nothing wrong with that. When you lose track of what you want, take a breath. Refocus. Remind yourself of your ultimate goal and what you need to do in order to get there.

FOR THE PARENTS

Before you spend time with your child, take a moment to breathe. Align yourself and your body. Don't feel guilty for taking a meditative moment during the day. It's a way of bringing yourself back to your goal: being a good parent.

As a parent, if you don't take enough time to breathe and focus, you might risk shutting your kid out. While they're talking, you might be all over the place, doing everything but listening to them. That's not being present in the moment. In that situation, you're not properly engaging with your child. You're only focusing on yourself, or things that, in that moment, shouldn't matter. Only the present moment matters, and if that moment is with your kid, that's where your focus should be.

CHAPTER 3

✳ ✳ ✳

WARM UP

LESSON: COORDINATION, COURAGE, PATIENCE
RULE: LISTEN AND NO CUTTING
GOAL: STRENGTH AND AGILITY

In any sport, warming up is important. Whenever you train, you need to warm up to prevent injury. If you've ever played sports, you already know this. It's what our coaches are always telling us—and they're right. A baseball player can't throw or swing the bat as well if he doesn't warm up first. However, warming up has other benefits as well, especially in the martial arts. Through a warm-up, you create flexibility, balance, and coordination. Don't skip your warm-up!

WHAT THE WARM-UP TEACHES US

Wait, the warm-up has a lesson? Of course! Everything

has a lesson. In some sports, the warm-up may be just for getting the body ready. But in martial arts, the warm-up is much more. It's a way of training the body and the mind as well as an opportunity to refine your martial arts skills.

COORDINATION, COURAGE, PATIENCE

There are lots of exercises you can do to warm up. You probably know several and maybe even have some favorites. In my gym, part of our warm-up is the scorpion walk. The scorpion walk works the core, upper body, and prevents back injury. It's also quite difficult.

Imagine doing a handstand, and then walking. With the help of a partner, that is the essence of the scorpion walk. You start with two hands on the floor, and one foot. Then imagining yourself as a scorpion with your feet being your tail, you throw the foot on the ground toward the sky to meet the other one.

Like I said—not easy. So why do we do it? Why don't we just run or do jumping jacks? Well, we do those things, too. But still, why would I make my students attempt such a difficult maneuver if all I was trying to do was get their muscles warm? Because it's not just the muscles I'm warming up. I'm also warming up and sharpening the connection between my students' minds and bodies.

This is why I say the three main lessons of the warm-up are coordination, courage, and patience.

It also takes coordination to get it right. It takes courage to perform a warm-up like the scorpion walk as the entire class watches. And it takes a lot of patience to build that coordination.

This is true of whatever exercise you do, even if it's something as seemingly simple as jumping jacks. Each warm-up exercise has its own benefit. And if we've practiced our meditation and are fully present, we can learn what each of the warm-up exercises has to teach us.

LISTENING

Nowadays, I don't think of things in terms of right or wrong. In any situation, there's a lesson you can easily learn if you listen, focus, and have the right information. If you choose not to listen, or if you lack focus, lessons will be much harder to learn.

That's especially true in the warm-ups. The warm-up is one of the best places to practice listening. Think about it. How many times have you been in a warm-up session and you were only half paying attention because it was just warm-up? It happens all the time. As we've seen, warm-ups have lessons to teach us. But we need to really be paying attention—really listening—in order to learn those lessons and gain those benefits.

STRENGTH AND AGILITY

Think in terms of rewards. When you do good things, good things will happen for you. For example, when we run, we practice coordination and balance. When we do the scorpion walk, we strengthen our core. Every time you do a jumping jack, there's a benefit of coordination. If you think of that benefit every time you do a jumping jack, you'll be more motivated to do more. A jumping jack is no longer just a boring movement. You're not just warming up, you're *practicing*. You're training your body.

Have the courage and patience to participate. Listen to what you need to be doing. And, remaining patient, reap the rewards.

HOW TO WARM UP

Warming up in martial arts is different from warming up in traditional sports. It's important to understand that difference and what it means to warm up as a martial artist.

It doesn't really matter what exercises you do. In fact, you might do the same routine as your school football team.

But *how* you approach those exercises and how you do them will be what separates you as a martial artist.

In a martial arts gym, I know I'm surrounded by people who support me. If I have a question or need help with a technique, I know I can always ask for it. Sometimes I learn lessons without even asking—if someone hits me in sparring or taps me out in jiu-jitsu, we instantly become best friends and show each other our best moves. Everyone is willing to help everyone else.

It's not the same in other sports. When I was playing basketball, I never felt like I could ask for help from my teammates. We were all on the same team, and yet I felt we were all competing with each other. Everyone wanted to be the best. Every player was playing for themselves. All anyone cared about was scoring, not helping each other succeed.

Imagine a basketball team warming up, passing the ball around. Suppose one of the players drops the ball or passes badly. If you've ever played a team sport, you know what a likely reaction is. That player will likely get made fun of or put down by his teammates for not being as skilled as they are. Does anyone step in to tell that player it's okay and help him with his technique? Unfortunately, in team sports, you often don't find that kind of helpful culture.

Typically, people training in a martial arts gym don't think of themselves as a team. Maybe that's because when we compete in tournaments, we compete as individuals. But in my gym and many others, we are a team—more so than the basketball team I once belonged to. People come in to train as individuals, but we are all there to support one another and grow together. We know that if one of us gets better, that pushes the rest of us to get better as well. That's a true team. That's how we warm each other up.

TIPS FOR WARMING UP

Like anything else in martial arts, there are always plenty of lessons to be learned in whatever we do. The warm-up is no different. By now it should be clear that warm-ups are not just activities your coach makes you do or that you should blow off. The warm-ups make you a better athlete and a better martial artist, and they make you more in tune with your own body.

EMBRACE THE STRUGGLE

Sometimes students assume that struggle means failure. It does not. Let me repeat: Struggling is not failure. In fact, struggle is the whole idea.

Let's say, for example, that a student finds himself grappling with an exercise—one that might not even be that difficult for other students. I encourage them to keep going and finish it. And if they do, I congratulate them because finishing an exercise is one step closer to achieving a larger goal.

The struggle provides an opportunity to learn the three most important lessons of warming up: coordination, courage, and patience. In order to finish the exercise, the student who was struggling had to have the *courage* to attempt it in front of the class with all the other students. They had to have the *patience* to keep trying, even though it was hard. And finally, because they stuck with it, their *coordination*, in addition to their ultimate goals of more strength and agility are improved because they embraced the struggle, fought through it, and got that much better through practice.

Whenever I want someone to demonstrate, I ask the class, "Who wants to do a good job, and who wants to be awesome?" I don't necessarily pick the one who will do it the best. I look for the kids who want to challenge themselves. I pick a kid who is good at listening, and who has strong focus and courage.

The students then demonstrate. Maybe it's something like the scorpion walk. Maybe they fall over, and that's okay. "This is what awesome looks like," I say. "It's okay if you fall over. I just want you to make sure that you have a smile on your face."

Guess what? Falling is good. It teaches you to be better next time. It takes courage to fall and try again. It takes patience to try over and over.

PRACTICE, PRACTICE...

I've had students who started classes with terrible balance. They'd try to do the scorpion walk and just drop down to the mat. That's okay, I've told them.

No one should feel discouraged—they should just feel like they need more practice. They need to realize they've chosen in, they need to be present, and they need to focus on their goal. When I communicate with my students, I always emphasize the word "improve." Every day, I want them to focus on getting better.

I tell my students the dojo isn't the only place they can practice their exercises. They can also practice at home. If they go home and do some extra practice, I promise them they will see the difference by the next week. It might not be a huge difference, but if they're improving, then that's what matters, because all those small improvements can add up to something big.

BACK TO FOCUS

The lessons I'm teaching in this book all weave together.

Some warm-ups, like the scorpion walk, are difficult, and I choose them because they're difficult. When something is difficult, you're forced to be focused. Therefore you're not just practicing movements, you're practicing focus. You're meditating with movement.

We live in a digital age. These days, kids are addicted to phones and tablets. I see this everywhere, and as a martial arts instructor—as someone who knows what it's like to see kids who are focused, present, and happy—it's sad for me to see it. When I go out to eat with my wife and kids, and I see a group of teenagers on their phones at the next table, I know not to be surprised when I see that they're texting each other even though they're sitting together. So many people just don't talk to each other anymore. We're not present. We're not focused.

Our warm-ups help us find that focus. Next time you're on your phone or tablet, consider putting it down. Then do some warm-ups.

CONFIDENCE

In my classes, I ask lots of questions. I want my gym to be an interactive place. By asking questions, I'm encouraging my students to participate.

For example, I might ask the kids who the current president is. One time a student raised his hand and answered "Hillary Clinton." While he got the answer wrong, I still praised him. I praised his confidence. "Everybody give him a round of applause. Excellent confidence. Good job for raising your hand up," I said.

The scorpion walk is hard. Just trying to do it with the fear of failing or falling makes it tough enough, let alone having an entire room look at you. It takes the same kind of confidence to do the scorpion walk as it does to raise your hand.

Courage leads to confidence.

FOLLOW—AND LEAD

Before anyone becomes a leader, they must learn how to follow. I was once a follower. When I was younger, I followed great martial artists. Slowly, my teachers saw that I demonstrated confidence. Now, I've become a teacher myself. I became a leader.

In a group of students, I try and recognize the strongest and most confident kids. The more I encourage them, the more they'll inspire the other kids in the group. In time, they can help those less confident students become more confident. They can turn their followers into leaders.

A WARMING UP STORY

Over the years, I've taught a lot of students. One thing I've learned is that kids are often afraid to jump. The reason is that they fear they'll be judged. When a kid feels like that, it's because they don't have enough data, information, or facts to see what's possible for them.

I remember one student in particular who struggled with jumping, although in his case, it wasn't just a matter of courage, it was also a matter of listening. The instructions were to frog jump from one side of the dojo to the other, but this student opted to crab walk.

One student told them they were doing the warm-up wrong, and I interjected.

I explained that the crab walk was indeed an effective exercise. It might not have been the drill we were using at that exact moment, but that doesn't make it wrong because the student was still displaying effort and determination.

Patience and courage often go hand in hand. The student knew how to frog jump, but hadn't mustered the courage to do it in front of his fellow students. So instead of telling him he was wrong, I gave him the gift of patience and pointed out the things he *was* doing right. It also gave him the courage and confidence he needed to have an honest and open conversation with me.

I asked him, "What do you need to improve?" And then, "Were you focusing completely when I was explaining the drill?"

I asked the questions without judgment, and he admitted that he and some other students were moving around, so they weren't focused when I explained the drill.

"If you focus, will you understand the drill?" I asked.

"Yes, I will," the student responded.

And after that, he did.

BEYOND THE DOJO

In life, every day is a drill. When we train, we warm up. When we live, we prepare. It's the same thing.

I wake up every morning at 4:00 a.m. Every time I wake up, I'm excited. Each new day is an opportunity to be better than I was yesterday. Every morning, I think about all the great things I have in my life. I think of my wife and my kids, for example. I ask myself: Did I spend enough time with them yesterday? Did I give them enough hugs and kisses? Did I say I love them enough?

As a martial artist, I have the opportunity to prepare to work toward my goals every day.

In life, if you don't strive toward your goals, you become lost. For example, what's the first thing you do when you wake up? So many people these days wake up and immediately look at their phone because they don't know what else to do with themselves. They have no goals, nothing to get them up and prepared.

It's up to you to prepare for your life. These are lessons you have to learn. If you want to be better tomorrow, prepare now. If you know you have to wake up at 7:00 a.m. to get to school on time, and you have a test, you won't be preparing yourself to do well if you stay up too late the night before.

Ask yourself: What do you want to accomplish tomorrow? How are you going to set up to accomplish those goals? Then, warm up.

Remember, the things you do today will affect your life tomorrow. Tomorrow is the consequence of today's choices. If you make a bad choice today, you can't play the victim tomorrow. In any situation, you can choose in or choose out. If you choose in, make sure you get ready.

FOR THE PARENTS

Warm up with your children. That doesn't mean you have to do jumping jacks or attempt scorpion walks with them. It means to prepare yourself for each interaction with your child. Be present in every warm-up, whatever parenting challenge you may be facing.

A lot of "warming up" in this sense, comes down to communication. If you're having a rough day, share that with your child before you get into anything else. It's important for kids to experience their parents' emotions. The more you open up as a parent, the more your kids will understand you and be able to empathize, and the more they'll learn about what it means to be an adult, which they will someday be.

Many parents tend to hide from their kids, perhaps because they don't think their kids are smart enough to understand adult problems. The funny thing is that kids are incredibly observant. You can't hide anything from them. Trying to hide things can only lead to problems.

All too often, kids see their parents lose their tempers, but have no idea why. While you might want to stay quiet and say nothing, it's important for your kids to understand why you're upset.

Share your challenges with your children. Warm up with

them. If you warm up with your kids, they will be much more likely to warm up with you. You can't expect your kids to open up about their challenges if you don't open up about yours. If you want your kids to share their lives with you, you have to be willing to share first.

As a parent you have to be honest with yourself and your child.

CHAPTER 4

* * *

STRETCHING

LESSON: NEGOTIATE, DON'T ARGUE
RULE: PARTICIPATE
GOAL: MENTAL AND PHYSICAL FLEXIBILITY

We've bowed in.

We've meditated.

We're warmed up.

Time to start punching and kicking things?

Not so fast. Next, we stretch.

WHAT STRETCHING TEACHES

When people stretch for the first time, they don't always

know what their process should be. They don't know what their bodies should be doing. That's why people tend to assume stretching is very difficult.

In reality, stretching isn't difficult as long as you understand *how* to do it and what it has to teach us.

NEGOTIATE

In training, it's inevitable that you'll come across certain movements you can't do. Some people can't do a side split. And because they can't do it, they'll often do one of two things: either they'll give up and never improve, or they'll force it and get injured (and, therefore, still not improve).

What they need to learn to do instead is negotiate.

Can't do a side split? No problem. The next step is to negotiate with your body to see *how much* you can do. The goal is to do enough to push your boundaries and improve, but not so much that you'll get injured.

In this sense, you're negotiating with your body. You're finding that place that's not too much and not too little. You're discovering what you can do that will help you improve and stay safe.

PARTICIPATE

When stretching, people have a tendency to tune in only to the pain or the resistance they feel in their body. Often, when people feel pain in their bodies, they hold their breath. If they hold their breath during a stretch, they lose the possibility to improve. Without realizing it, they've opted out of the stretch. They're no longer really participating. They're just holding themselves in pain, telling themselves they're stretching.

In my gym, we often count when we stretch. That's my little trick. When we count through a stretch out loud, people are subconsciously breathing. When you focus your breathing (remember the chapter on meditation?), you're totally in the present moment.

As an instructor, I want everybody to participate in my classes. I make sure everyone in my gym does the same movement. I want my students to engage with me. If they're not participating, they're not engaged. They're disconnected, and they lose themselves. When people become lost, they give up.

I don't want anyone to give up. I want everyone to participate.

Not everyone is going to drop right down into the side splits. Some people might not ever. That's okay. That's not what flexibility is about.

Flexibility is about improvement. It's about negotiating with your body. It's about participating and engaging with your body. It's about learning that not only have you become more flexible physically, but that through learning to negotiate with yourself, you've learned to become more flexible with yourself.

HOW TO STRETCH

Often, people don't fully understand the benefits of stretching, why it's important, or how it works.

Let's say someone is bending over, attempting to touch their toes. Many people, as soon as they feel that stretch in the back of their leg, think, "That's enough." They think that's what stretching is. They're right that this physical experience is part of stretching, but it's not everything.

Stretching is designed to expose you to your body. It can make you more aware of yourself.

The first step toward stretching correctly is knowing how to breathe. The second step is to connect the breathing with the stretching. Again, imagine someone standing up and trying to touch their toes. When a lot of people do this, they forget to breathe. They're reaching, they're trying, but they're not breathing. They're executing a bad—and potentially dangerous—stretch.

Picture it this way: Your stomach is like a balloon. When it blows up, you can only blow it up so much. When it's deflated, the balloon is flat. Greater movement is now possible. Often when people are stretching, they're forcing their bodies into positions instead of breathing and allowing their bodies to find those positions with less effort.

It's simple. All you have to do is breathe in and breathe out. In my classes, I make my students sit down and put both feet in front of them. I tell everyone to breathe in and breathe out. No fighting the body. And when we begin to stretch, I remind them to just keep breathing and negotiate the point in the stretch that is right for them.

TIPS FOR STRETCHING

Stretching is crucial for your physical body. Stretching will help you live longer and perform better. It can be very easy, however, to stretch in ways that are unhealthy. Here are some things to keep in mind as you incorporate stretching into your life.

TAKE IT SLOW

Every time you train, think about your goal. Remember what you want to accomplish with every movement. You can't go into the gym expecting results if you don't set any goals for yourself.

If you have never stretched in your life, your first goal might be to understand your body. The more you educate yourself, the more you can treasure your body.

DON'T COMPETE

When people walk into the dojo, they have a tendency to look around the room, figuring out who's best. People always try and compare themselves to others. Instead of focusing on themselves, they focus on others.

This isn't healthy. It creates a negative mindset. It makes someone feel like they aren't flexible enough or good enough. They sabotage their own training because what they should be focused on is their own improvement.

SMALL GOALS

Ask yourself: how do you want to improve your flexibility? A lot of people don't consider making small benchmarks as a way to achieve their ultimate goal. This can be harmful because the ultimate goal is probably a long way off. If you want to do the splits and are only halfway there, it's a long road ahead.

Think of it like getting a black belt. You don't do that overnight. You don't do that for *years*. But along the way there are other belts—other benchmarks—to guide you and help you track your progress. They're also something to be proud of. Set benchmarks for your flexibility and enjoy the journey.

A STRETCHING STORY

I often negotiate with my kids. For example, I recently told my daughter I didn't mind if she watched TV as long as she finished all of her reading for school first. Once she did her reading, I said, she could watch TV for half an hour. After half an hour, she had to read or play with her brother. "Why do I have to do that?" she asked.

I explained to her that you have to create tasks and set goals if you want to get anything done in life. As an adult, I create goals for myself. In school, you get tasks set for you that you have to complete before you go back to school. (This, as you know, is called homework.) If my daughter chose to watch TV instead of doing her reading, she would lose a lot of time and have to catch up on her studying later.

In the end, my daughter did her homework first. When she

finished her homework, we agreed that she could watch half an hour of TV. About ten minutes in, I reminded her of our agreement. We confirmed that she would watch exactly thirty minutes of TV.

When you make an agreement, it's important to underline it. By guiding my daughter and communicating with her, I helped her understand the situation. That way, she was able to take responsibility for her own tasks.

Now imagine you're watching TV, and your mom tells you to turn it off and clean your room. She might threaten you, as a lot of parents tend to do. You'll probably do what she says, but you'll doubt yourself. You won't have a lot of confidence. Nobody really likes conflict, so you might withdraw from your mom. The second you become withdrawn, you lose the ability to learn.

If your mom asks you to clean your room and you don't want to, the first thing to do is ask yourself *why* you're resisting. Next, I recommend you respond this way: "Mom, at this second, I don't want to clean my room because I'm watching TV. Is there any way I can do it after I finish the show?"

With that response, your mom understands *why* you're resisting doing as she says. If you explain yourself properly and respectfully, there won't be a conflict. A fire won't have flames if no one is pouring gasoline over it.

Also, when you're feeling upset, check in with yourself. How are you breathing? How are you feeling in the moment? How can you change that feeling?

Again, you have a choice to choose in or out. If you choose in, you might choose to have a fight with your parents. That's a consequence of your choice, not a reward. For example, you might get a toy taken away.

Alternatively, you could choose out. That means you join hands, communicate, and compromise with your parents. Obviously, that's a much better result. You're happy, and your parents are happy.

When you perform tasks that help the house look better and you learn to communicate with your parents, not only do you show your love for your parents, but you show your love for yourself. You quickly learn to forget anger and negative emotions.

BEYOND THE DOJO

When we create flexibility in martial arts, we learn how to adapt to situations better in real life.

Imagine I'm sparring with a student, and they throw a kick to the stomach. That he can do this is good, but if he's more flexible, he has more options. He can also throw a kick to the head. Now, if kicking to the body isn't an option, it's okay. He has others.

The same pattern applies in life. Outside of the gym, there are so many situations in which you have to be flexible. Say I'm driving to someone's house, and there's construction on the road. The wrong way to deal with this is to play the victim—to get angry and act as though there are no other options and the world is out to get me (I'd probably be holding my breath through all this, too). The right way to deal with this situation is to be flexible and find an alternate route.

When you're faced with an unexpected situation, you have to be able to adapt.

MENTAL FLEXIBILITY

It's important to practice flexibility in all areas of your life. If I'm watching TV, and my wife asks me to take the trash out, I have some options. I can choose to resist, for example, and tell her that I'm watching a good show and that I'm not going to take the trash out.

However, I can also choose to be flexible. I can negotiate—and I don't even have to necessarily negotiate with my wife. I can negotiate with myself. I can think about how I can do what I need to do (take the trash out) while still not totally giving up the thing I want. Maybe I can pause what I'm watching. Or maybe the show is almost over, and I can promise to take the trash out as soon as it ends and then follow through on that promise. Or I could even miss a bit of my show and realize it's not the end of the world.

I can meet somewhere in the middle. I can push myself beyond the boundaries of my comfort zone, just like in a stretch. I can negotiate. I can meet others where they are to improve relationships.

FLEXIBILITY WITH YOURSELF

If I'm ever feeling upset, I ask myself what my goal is in that moment. And in that moment, I have to make a decision. Do I want to be happy that day? Or do I want to be a victim?

Happiness is a choice. If you choose to be happy, that means finding solutions for yourself to be happy. For example, if I'm feeling upset, I might go for a run or to the gym to cheer myself up.

On the other hand, I can choose to do nothing—because doing nothing, even though it doesn't feel like it, is a choice. And if I choose to do nothing, I have to accept the consequences that come with that.

Just like participating in a tough stretch, it's my responsibility to make the choice to do the difficult thing or not.

LIFE BENCHMARKS

I'm constantly thinking about my goals. Personally, I like to live by minutes, so I define my goals for each minute.

If you have high expectations, you risk setting goals that you won't be able to achieve. As a result, you might start to feel like a failure. To avoid feeling like a failure, know your benchmarks, just like in a stretch. Maybe you're not able to do a split today, but are you stretching a bit further than you were last week? Good, you've hit a benchmark. Keep going.

Your benchmark in life might be an emotional feeling. For example, imagine a person who is prone to road rage. First, they have to recognize where they are emotionally. In this case, they're not very flexible. By recognizing this, they can start to give themselves benchmarks. Perhaps they still get upset at other drivers, but they're no longer shouting. That's a benchmark. Next, perhaps they find they're speeding less and driving less aggressively. That's another benchmark—more growth. Before long, they might find themselves rarely getting upset, allowing other drivers to go before them at four-way stops, and stopping in the street to let pedestrians cross.

That kind of growth doesn't happen overnight. But bench-marks can get you there.

THE FOUR CS

In life, I remain flexible by remembering the four Cs: com-munication, compassion, compromise, and commitment.

You have to communicate with others to be flexible. Com-munication means not only expressing your ideas, but also truly listening to someone else.

Next, you must have compassion for others. You must truly care. You must remember that it isn't all about you. Seeing the other side and caring about it is essential in life.

Having listened with compassion, you must now find a way to compromise. If you truly felt compassionate, then this shouldn't be too hard. Compromise is usually much easier than we think it is.

Lastly, you must commit to that compromise. You must follow through. You do that, and you'll be happier. So will the others in your life.

FOR THE PARENTS

When parents ask their kids to do something, they don't

typically set goals for them. Instead, they set demands. For example, "Clean up your room" is what I call a demand. A better way of phrasing this request is, "I know you're watching TV right now, but the commercial is coming up. When it does, would you please get up and clean your room? You'll be done by the time the commercial ends, so you won't miss anything." In the second example, the parent is being flexible and setting a specific goal.

I also encourage parents to have a little more flexibility. Even though you probably want a task done right away, demands don't always work. Before you deal with your kids, you have to know where they stand. You have to apply the four Cs.

Turn the tables. Imagine if you were watching a good show and your kids asked you to do something. I bet you'd tell them to wait a minute, and you'd expect them to wait. If so, why would you expect your kids to react any differently when you ask them the same question? After all, you're the one setting the example.

When it comes down to it, kids and adults want exactly the same thing. In today's society, the problem is that we fail to communicate properly. The less we communicate, the less parents can connect with their children.

Everyone is quick to blame TV and other technology, but the reality is that parents don't communicate enough with their kids. They don't have the compassion that comes from truly listening to what's important to their kids to be able to reach fair compromises that both sides can commit to.

Parenting is tough. Take it from me. Breathe. Be flexible.

CHAPTER 5

✳ ✳ ✳

BASICS

LESSON: ALIGNMENT
RULE: SYNCHRONIZE WITH OTHERS AS ONE
GOAL: EXPRESS YOURSELF

Often, your body has no problem handling pain. But your mind does. That's why it's so important to train your mind *before* your body.

The basics drill conditions your body. The more your body gets hit, the more you learn to deal with pain. Your body becomes tough.

In the basics drill, we start to bring all of the components together. I recommend mastering each of these practices on your own before you begin working with a partner.

WHAT THE BASICS TEACH

ALIGNMENT

Alignment is about the connection of your breathing to your body. To be aligned is to have your breathing in tune with your heart.

As I said in chapter 2, the reason many people meditate is because they want to clear their mind. In my opinion, it's impossible to completely clear your mind. That's why instead, I aim for alignment.

All my training, even my sparring, is based on my breathing. If I find myself breathing heavily, I know my body will start to tense up. But if I breathe calmly and slowly, my body won't tense up. I'll move more fluidly. I'll be aligned.

As a martial artist, I have to find that alignment, no matter the situation. Sometimes this is easy. Other times it's a little bit harder. Think of alignment like stretching. Some days you can get into a stretch with no problem. Other days your body just won't stretch the way you want it to. On those harder days, I know I need to slow down, breathe, and work on becoming one with my body. I need to become aligned.

SYNCHRONIZE

In my gym, we practice together as a team. I get my students to synchronize so they're all yelling together as they perform a move.

"Everybody focus," I tell them. "When you hear the word go, I want you to yell together."

We practice this synchronization over and over again. Every time, I encourage my students to be louder and stronger. When the whole class connects, the sound of all those voices booms and echoes. It's an impressive, heart-stopping sound. It makes us realize how strong we are when we're truly working as a team. When we're truly aligned.

EXPRESS YOURSELF

If you don't know what it means to express yourself, practice this exercise.

First, I want you to close your eyes. Think of yourself being happy. Now punch and yell out the word "happy." How do you feel? Do you feel excited? Do you feel happy? Did you have fun?

Now, imagine that you're mad at somebody. Punch and yell again. How do you feel now? You probably feel pretty angry. Try punching again, but this time think about your speed.

Which feeling inspires you to have the best workout? In class, a lot of my students like the angry feeling better. I aim to retrain that. I want my students to have a positive attitude while they're training.

I know your life is already challenging enough. You have your own routines and your own struggles. Maybe you frequently fight with your parents. My job as a teacher isn't to make your life any harder. My job is to help you see possibilities. I want you to see that happiness and positivity are possible.

Sometimes you just have to force yourself to find it.

...Even if It Means Crying

Seeing that happiness and positivity are possible doesn't mean you have to be happy all the time. In my gym, I have tissues everywhere. If my students ever feel like they need to cry, they're welcome to cry.

I try to say this in a fun way, because no one should be embarrassed to cry. It's fine for anyone to cry, as long as they understand that they still have to train. "If you need to cry, get it out," I tell my students. "When you finish, you can go back to training and having fun."

The reason I let my students cry is because I understand

their situation. I understand where they are and how they want to be treated.

Always be aware of how you want to be treated and let this guide your decisions about how you're going to treat others. These practices always start at home. If you want someone to treat you right, treat them right as well.

Negative to Positive

Think of the last time you were mad at something. Practice making the sound you make when you're angry. How does your belly feel?

In martial arts, we use that angry energy in a positive way. You can take that negative energy and channel it into something positive, such as protecting your body.

Whenever you get mad, channel that negative energy toward your training. That way, you use that bad energy for good, and nobody gets hurt.

Learning to channel that energy can take practice. At my gym, I deliberately have punching bags set up all over the place. If kids come in feeling really angry, I send them to the punching bags so they can practice punching and kicking. I tell them to yell as loud as they need to. The only rule is that they must yell something positive. No matter how angry someone is feeling, I always want my gym to have a positive atmosphere.

They yell words like "Awesome!" and "Cool!" as they practice punching, and I guide them. At first, some of them struggle. Slowly, I watch them punch harder and harder. Their punches become more and more connected. Suddenly they let go of their sadness or anger. At that point, I give them a clap to acknowledge that they found themselves.

They are aligned.

Everyone loses themselves sometimes. That's okay. If you ever need to find your way, the dojo is the place to do that. Whatever challenges my students are going through, I make sure they know that I am there to support them and the dojo is a safe place to work through their problems.

HOW TO DRILL THE BASICS

I always tell my students that the basics are the foundation for everything. Whether at home or in the dojo, it's important to remember what the foundation is that is holding everything up. At home, for example, we might be focused on a lot of things that seem big, but aren't when we compare them to the basics. We might be worried about what our parents let us do, our curfew, how much TV we get to watch, or when we get to hang out with our friends, or how much homework we have to do. But underneath all that is a stronger foundation that affects everything. The basics of your home are your parents and your relationship with them.

Just like at home, the basics in martial arts can be hard to see and easy to forget. That's why we take the time to train them.

It's easy to get caught up in the fun techniques of martial arts, but if we forget to train the basics, we lose the technique. So we always take time to drill the basic positions, like horse stance and the defense stance, and we focus on the transitional movements between them. When we move into techniques, we take time to focus on the transitions between our lunges and kicks, not just the techniques themselves. We slow down to understand how each movement complements the next, and how everything fits together.

TIPS FOR THE BASICS

If there's one thing I hope you've learned so far, it's that there's nothing "basic" about the basics.

Like anything else, we could just go through the motions, but the basics teach us important lessons about alignment, synchronization, and self-expression.

To practice, here are some tips that can help you master the basics.

VISUALIZE IT

Think about how your body works when you perform certain movements. For example, how is your breathing in line with your kicks or jumps?

Don't just do the movements. Think about them. See yourself doing them. Think about the entire movement of your body, all the way down to your breath.

Now, move.

SHADOW BOX

When you're practicing the basics drill, find a mirror. We have a mirror in my gym for this exact reason. Look at your own reflection. As you practice, think about punching yourself in the mirror.

Say you're throwing a straight punch. Your target is your head. See the target. Punch the target.

This is called shadow boxing. A lot of people have a hard time shadow boxing. They don't see their targets and start to doubt themselves.

Give yourself a target. Let that target be you. You'll not only have something to aim for, but you'll also become more familiar with your technique and the way you uniquely move.

START SIMPLE

When you're starting out, practice stationary punches. In a stationary punch, you're more likely to see your alignment. Punch your hand out and check your form. Make sure your arm is straight. Repeat that punch a couple of times. Hold your hand out. You can work on resistance later. For now, focus on your form.

Once you've had enough slow practice, you can work on speed. Punch, yell out, and stop as fast as you can. After you punch, bring your hand back fast so you don't get stuck in traffic. (Traffic is when your hand comes out while your other hand stays where it was.) No one likes being stuck in traffic. When you punch your hand out, bring it back as fast as you can. Whatever you throw out has to come back in. Keep your posture up. Look straight ahead.

I make sure to demonstrate this exercise in my classes.

DITCH THE MIRROR—WHEN YOU'RE READY

Once you've practiced looking at yourself in the mirror,

close your eyes. Now return to visualization, but this time, visualize punching yourself in the mirror.

Your goal is to close your eyes and see an image before you. When you see the image, your goal is to execute the same punch that you would if your eyes were open.

You might be wondering why I tell you to practice punches with your eyes closed. When you close your eyes, you train your brain to see what it wants to see. Eventually, you'll train your brain enough to see your opponent even when you can't really see him.

BREATHE!

As you know, breathing is the most basic movement you need for martial arts. After you master your breathing, you need to be in tune with how you move your body. When you stretch, be aware of how your body moves. Use your breathing to empower your movements.

BE CONSISTENT

You won't see the improvement you want if your training is scattered. Practice your basics, including meditation, on a regular schedule. The more consistent you are, the more you will improve.

A BASICS STORY

If you want a relationship with someone else, you have to build a relationship with yourself first. You have to be the best version of you. You have to figure out what the basics of your life and your character are. Before you can take care of anyone else, you have to take care of yourself.

I once had a staff member who worked with me for about a year. I found out he was cheating on his girlfriend. Now, I have five rules in my dojo: effort, etiquette, character, sincerity, and self-control The third rule, character, is the most important. By being dishonest, this employee was not living up to his potential character. If he chose to be honest and focus on his character, then lots of other problems—with his girlfriend, with the other girl, with me, with the dojo—would all disappear. The basics are what everything in our lives stand on. If your basics are strong, so is everything else.

I told this employee that if he worked with me while cheating on his girlfriend, he was breaking the integrity of my gym. I gave him two options. Either he could continue to cheat on her and not work with me, or he could tell her the truth and break up with her. All I wanted was for him to be honest with himself. As long as he was honest with himself, I said, I could continue working with him.

"That's my personal life," he said.

Although this was true, I asked him what kind of character he was demonstrating for the students.

In the end, this employee didn't care. At least, not enough to fess up and be honest, and take responsibility. That was poor character.

I let him go.

BEYOND THE DOJO

Every person's life is made up of simple individual components. In other words, basics. Communication is one example. Think about it: If you avoid communication, everything else in your life will fail. But if you're focused on being a good communicator, a lot of problems can take care of themselves.

In my life, I focus on communication, love, care, and inspiration. Every day, I strive to be a role model for my children, my community, and my neighborhood, and the basics play a role in all my relationships. To have a healthy and happy relationship with my wife, for example, I focus on communicating with her about things that matter. I make sure not to forget her birthday, our anniversary, or the first day we met. As a husband, those are the basic details I need to recall and acknowledge to help my wife care about and love me.

To become strong in whatever you're doing, figure out what the basics of your life are. Then be consistent in practicing those basics and prioritize them.

FOR THE PARENTS

I recognize that everyone has a different style of parenting. But I think that some basics—communication, honesty, commitment—are fairly universal.

As a parent, suppose you have to go somewhere for work for an extended period of time. It's your responsibility to communicate with your kids and ensure their basic needs will still be met when you're away. If I'm ever going somewhere, I ask my kids how I can make sure that I show them I love them. How can I show them I care?

I ask these questions because I'm genuinely interested in their answers.

Kids like to ask questions too. If you openly communicate with your kids, they start to ask questions back. When I'm going away, my kids ask how they can support me at home, and I give them a list of things they can do.

CHAPTER 6

✳ ✳ ✳

PARTNER UP

LESSON: COMMUNICATION

RULE: PARTICIPATE

GOAL: FULLY ENGAGE WITH OTHERS

Now it's time to practice with another person.

Whenever you partner up with someone, remember your previous lessons. Acknowledge them. Be present with them. Engage with them. If you know you're going to be partnered with someone, it might be a good idea to shake their hand and introduce yourself.

In other words, bow. Choose in. Commit.

WHAT PARTNERING UP TEACHES

When we partner up, we practice all kinds of things. It's a

time to isolate certain movements, punches, kicks, blocks, or weapon disarms. We might use pads or just go slow, using each other's bodies.

We are, of course, learning the moves. But partnering up gives us a chance to learn even more lessons about our technique, how to work together, and how to be good martial artists.

COMMUNICATION

All partners should communicate with each other. And that communication should be positive. It should be inspiring and empowering.

A great way for partners to empower each other is to offer encouragement. Imagine you're blocking your partner's punches. You can ask your partner to punch a little bit faster so you can improve your blocking if you feel like you're ready. Don't be afraid to ask for what you want. And don't be afraid to say what you think, either.

Communication isn't just verbal. For example, eye contact counts as communication, too. To inspire you to block well, your partner might start the drill by punching slow. Over time, as the two of you improve, your partner might start punching a little faster and a little stronger.

That's his way of communicating to you that he thinks you're ready for more.

PARTICIPATION

Partnering encourages initiative. If no one picks you for a partner, you have the opportunity to choose one for yourself. Either you can be proactive and take action, or you can wait and hope somebody comes to you.

Don't miss that opportunity.

"Get a partner," I tell my class. And often, I see a lot of people standing still, desperately hoping someone will come to them.

If you are one of these people, challenge yourself to take the initiative. Approach someone you think will help you improve and ask to be their partner.

When you wait around for someone to ask you, chances are that the person who finally approaches you lacks confidence. They weren't willing to take initiative right away. Like you, they didn't want to take a risk. On the other hand, if you take initiative right away, you prove that you're a risk-taker—and everyone wants to be partnered with a risk-taker.

FULL ENGAGEMENT

Whenever you're sparring or dealing with a partner, you have to learn to engage with that person. You have to pay attention so you can understand how that person moves. Imagine your partner steps forward and punches. How can you defend it? What if you don't know the distance between yourself and your opponent? How are you going to defend yourself? Partner drills teach not only communication, but also engagement.

If you and your partner aren't engaged, not only are you being bad partners and not getting the most out of the drill—it can be dangerous! If you're holding the pads and not paying attention, your partner might punch you in the face.

Don't let that happen. In addition to danger, that's just plain embarrassing.

Now, imagine another scenario where you're completely engaged with your partner. You've taken the time to discover things about each other. In this drill, you're practicing kicks. You've trained with this person before, so you already know that they have a high and fast kick. They're also quite flexible, so you have to hold the pad high.

As the drill goes on, you could try lifting the pad up higher to inspire your partner to kick better. That helps increase their flexibility and power. They know you're a risk-taker, and they see that you're challenging them. Now they're challenging themselves to kick even higher.

Do you notice how this is a much more positive partnership? That's the power of engagement.

HOW TO PARTNER UP

Just do it.

You have to communicate. You have to participate. You have to be engaged. That requires action.

When it's time to partner up, it's time to be a leader. Grab a partner. Be the first one. Show the class what engagement looks like. Show your partner how it feels to be chosen.

When it's time to find a partner—find a partner!

TIPS FOR BEING A GOOD PARTNER

We know we have to communicate and be engaged, but what else can we do to be good partners? Here are some tips that will help you—and your partner—get the most out of partner drilling.

TAKE OWNERSHIP

"Who runs the class?"

This is a question I ask my students at the beginning of our lessons. Usually, their answer is the same.

"You run the class," they say.

I shake my head.

"I'm not running the class," I tell them. "You are." Sure, I'm the teacher, but it's *their* class. I can do my best to teach and inspire, but at the end of the day, it's up to them to get the most out of it. It's *their* class. That's the power a student has.

What are you going to do with that power?

ASK FOR FEEDBACK

Say you're participating in a high-block drill. Throughout training, you've been wondering whether your high block is strong or not. Before you begin the exercise, you could ask your partner for some feedback. They can tell you if your block is strong. Providing feedback is another example of great communication between two partners. (More on this in chapter 9.)

These days, people are scared to ask for feedback or

advice from others. In reality, nobody's going to judge you if you ask for help. People are nowhere near as mean as you might think.

ASK QUESTIONS

You've heard it before, and it's true: there's no such thing as a stupid question.

Imagine you and I are partnered up, and we're practicing punching techniques. As we're punching, I notice that your technique could be improved. Giving feedback is good (more on this also in chapter 9), but sometimes we risk offending our partner. Or sometimes we might know something is off with our partner's technique—or our own—but we're just not sure what. That's when it's time to raise your hand.

By asking for help, you're not just helping you or your partner. Both of you can learn from the conversation with your teacher. Beyond that, by raising your hand, you're also being a leader. You're demonstrating—and teaching your classmates—humility by showing how easy and beneficial it is to simply ask when you don't know.

A PARTNERING UP STORY

Let me tell you a true story.

I was once working with a staff member at my dojo who didn't understand what he was supposed to do. When I gave him honest feedback, he got offended. He got so offended that he started a rumor about me.

As his employer—a kind of partner—I had a choice. Either I could be upset with him, or I could learn to be a better person and forgive him. In the end, I forgave him. I didn't argue with the person. He left the dojo and we both moved forward.

But to resolve the situation, we needed to communicate.

I thought the best way for me to communicate all my thoughts regarding this situation was to send an email. "I want to let you know, I forgive you," I wrote. "And I wish you the best." Although he felt uncomfortable when he saw me, he also wished me the best.

Many people assume that they have to get upset when they face a problem. But why? Will getting upset serve you in any way?

In life, some people play the victim while others don't. Some people take initiative right away, while others take a little longer. There's nothing wrong with that.

In this case, even though it took this person a bit longer

to come around, I'm glad I used my skills in being a good partner. I stayed calm, engaged, and communicated. If I'd just gotten angry, he wouldn't have had the chance to grow. By being a good partner, I was able to help that person move further along their path in a positive way.

BEYOND THE DOJO

Partnering teaches you about engagement with the people in your life.

Picture the scene. My wife tells me to clean the house. I acknowledge her request and agree to do it. However, I don't tell her when I'm going to clean up. She gets upset thinking I ignored her request to clean.

At that point, I have two options. Number one, I can forget about the situation and be in denial, refusing to communicate with her. That might be an option, but it's not a solution. To find a solution, you need to communicate, compromise, and commit.

If you choose to be in a relationship or partnership— whether that means you're partnered with a boyfriend or girlfriend, a boss, a coworker, a friend, anyone—you need to put work into it. You need to be engaged. If you're not willing to put hard work into a relationship and be honest, how do you expect your life to be better?

In any kind of relationship, you can give up. You can focus on challenges instead of solutions, and you can play the victim. But where does that get you? The more you do that, the more you fade away from your own relationship.

On the other hand, the more you communicate, engage, and commit, the better your relationships will become. The better your relationships become, the better your life will be. This is what partnering drills can help you learn.

It's also important to remember that outside the dojo you have control over who you're partnered with. If you're spending time with people who drink and do drugs, all you have to do is stop spending time with them. You can bow out and choose another partner. It takes the same initiative and confidence you learned in the dojo.

FOR THE PARENTS

No matter where you live or what situation you're in, there's so much support out there. All you have to do is ask.

I teach two kids who live in the same town, not too far away from each other. Both kids would come to karate, but one kid's dad wouldn't have time to pick his kid up. He could easily have asked the other parent for that favor, but he was too proud to ask for support. He was resistant to ask for any help.

In that situation, what is the dad teaching his child? A lack of community. He was also teaching that communication isn't important—that it's better to keep your thoughts, and needs, and emotions to yourself.

In my opinion, if we live on this Earth, we are a community. It doesn't matter if I drive a cheap car and you drive a Ferrari. We are all part of the same community.

The reason people are so afraid to ask for support is because they assume they'll be rejected or judged. How can you assume the answer is no if you haven't even asked the question? Anyone who works in sales knows that a no is not a big deal. If you get a no, you move on to the next person. If the next person says no, you try someone else. Eventually, you will get a yes.

If more communities—and the parents in those communities—were willing to work together, we would easily find solutions to our problems.

CHAPTER 7

✳ ✳ ✳

SELF-DEFENSE

LESSON: PAY ATTENTION
RULE: ENGAGE
GOAL: CONTROL THE OUTCOME

Imagine that someone has a knife and they're coming toward you, ready to attack. With that knife, they have the opportunity to control you. But with the right kind of training, you have the ability to control them.

In many situations, people know they have the ability to take control, but they either don't want to or are afraid to. We train in self-defense so that when the situation calls for it, we have both the desire and ability to take control.

WHAT SELF-DEFENSE TEACHES

If you haven't practiced self-defense, taking control of

situations probably isn't second nature for you yet. I love martial arts because they can teach you how. But you have to train yourself to get there.

PAY ATTENTION

How many times have you been told by teachers or parents to pay attention? Well, guess what? It's good advice!

What you need to develop as a martial artist is situational awareness. Think about where you are right now. Are you really aware? Do you know how many people are around you? If you had to suddenly exit the room, would you know where to go?

Because we're all so addicted to our phones these days, it's easy to be distracted. That can make you a target for anyone who might want to do you harm, but it's also no way to go through life. Wake up! Pay attention to what's around you and who's around you.

Take some time to practice this. Walk around your school or neighborhood with a higher awareness. Look around. Notice things. Notice how good it feels to be aware of your surroundings and situation.

ENGAGE

A lesson we've seen before: By engaging in class and in life, we practice the art of being active rather than passive. In a self-defense situation, you cannot afford to be a spectator. You must engage! You must be fully present.

Imagine that attacker with the knife again. Now imagine a bad day you had in the dojo where you were tired or distracted, and just not performing your best. Is that how you want to respond now, when someone is attacking you and it counts? How you train will ultimately determine how you act.

Therefore, when it's time to train, it's time to engage.

CONTROL THE OUTCOME

To control the outcome of a fight, there are different factors you have to take into consideration. If your partner is stronger than you or weighs more than you, be prepared for them to punch harder. As soon as you look at your partner, you should have an idea of how to control the outcome of the training.

This is related to situational awareness, except now that awareness has narrowed just to the person you have to deal with.

It's important to remember that a self-defense situation is not a sparring session in the gym! This isn't the time to play loose, or get creative, or try out new techniques. It's the time to learn what you have to do to control outcomes. This is why, in my dojo, we'll have days when we're trying something new and other days, such as when we're preparing for a competition, when we're focusing on what we already know works for us. Our knowledge and skill should always be evolving. But we should also know what our best techniques are so that when the time comes, we know what we can rely on.

HOW TO TRAIN SELF-DEFENSE

The first thing we focus on in self-defense training is communication. It is always important to communicate with your partner, but it is especially important in self-defense training because we may be using dangerous movements or training weapons. As we'll see, there are different phases in our self-defense training and if we don't know how our partner is expecting us to attack or vice versa, someone could get injured. If we're practicing disarming someone with a weapon, for example, and they move too fast before we're ready, we risk getting hit with that weapon.

Once we've communicated, we move on to the first phase of self-defense training: memorization. In a real-life situation, if you hesitate, it could cost you your life. Therefore we train our movements in self-defense situations until we don't need to think about them.

Once we don't have to think about them, we can move on to the next aspect of self-defense training: flow. You must learn to flow with your partner in training. Again, there can be no hesitation. Now that the movements have become automatic, they must be smooth and seamless, as though they are happening on their own as your partner moves. You can train self-defense movements by yourself, but at some point you must train with another person to develop timing, which is crucial to learning how to flow.

The third and final step is not only memorizing and flowing, but being fully engaged with our partner and our own breathing and posture. This is the phase when everything becomes aligned.

TIPS FOR SELF-DEFENSE TRAINING

REPETITION IS KEY

Imagine you're in a martial arts class, and your teacher instructs your partner to practice leaning forward and grabbing your neck. When someone grabs your throat, you can either block the hand coming to grab you or turn your body out. Your teacher tells you to practice turning your body out.

The first time you turn, you practice the move. Just the movement, nice and slow. The second time, you can execute the movement a little bit faster. If your partner is engaged, they should inspire you by giving you the amount of resistance you need.

After this, try the move again. And again. Over and over.

While some drills can feel repetitive, there's a reason we do a lot of repetition in martial arts. The goal is for these moves to become second nature. This happens only when you build muscle memory, and you can only build muscle memory through repetition.

BUILDING MUSCLE MEMORY

When you fight, the movements should come instinctively. Say you practice how to do a front kick every single day. Eventually, your body will perform a front kick without you even having to think about it.

If you have to think about your movements during a fight, you end up losing yourself.

In life, there are certain skills you've mastered without even realizing it. When you wake up in the morning, chances are, the first thing you do is go to the bathroom. You could probably walk to your bathroom with your eyes closed. Think about the way you brush your teeth or comb your hair—how you've done it over and over and, through the years, have made only small tweaks as you continue to do it over and over.

Chances are you've never thought of your morning routine this way before. And that's the whole point—to not have to think about it. Imagine being able to handle an attacker without really thinking. That's the power of muscle memory.

BEING A GOOD PARTNER

When you're practicing self-defense with a partner, your goal is to subdue them so they don't hurt you. At the same time, you shouldn't hurt them. Your goal is to execute and practice the moves while still training safely. In other words, don't be selfish. If you only care about yourself, you could end up hurting your partner.

The more you help and inspire people, the more they will want to be around you and return the favor.

SHARPENING YOUR WEAPONS

You're practicing straight punches with me as your partner. You practice ten times. The first time, you can't reach me. The second time, you try a little harder, but you're still misjudging the distance a bit. By the third or fourth time, you learn the distance and are able to reach me. This is an example of sharpening your technique.

When you sharpen your technique, you sharpen your weapons. The more you practice a technique, the more small adjustments you make, the sharper your weapon is. It's no different than continually sharpening a sword, making it just a bit sharper with every pass of a whetstone. As a martial artist, your body is your weapon. Keep it sharp.

BEING CONSISTENT

Imagine a boy who's trying to impress a girl. If he delivers flowers to her door at the same time every day, that girl will be impressed. She might even start to fall for the boy. In this situation, the boy is taking consistent action steps toward his goal.

Instead of delivering flowers every day, imagine another boy brings flowers once. The girl doesn't hear from him for a couple of weeks. Out of nowhere, he asks her out to dinner.

Who do you think the girl is going to be more likely to go on a date with? The one who's consistent and unwavering, or the one who just shows up sometimes?

When you practice something consistently, you develop a flow. When you get your body into a flow state, it becomes much easier to react. Your body knows the movements. They've become second nature, and when they need to be called upon, they're ready.

A SELF-DEFENSE STORY

In 1999, I was working as security staff for a nightclub. One night, two customers got into an argument. One of the other staff members came out and confronted them. He was so focused on those two he didn't stop to think—to pay attention—to who else might be involved. A friend of one of the men who was arguing was standing by and stabbed the employee while he was focused on the arguing men.

Thankfully, the stabbing wasn't fatal. But the incident did teach me a valuable lesson about knowing my surroundings. Now, in any situation, I aim to create distance from those around me so I can fully engage and understand where I am. If I'm not engaged with my surroundings, I could get hurt at any second.

If you take anything from this story, it should be to know your surroundings. Pay attention. Even if you're dealing with just one person, be aware of the people and environment around you.

BEYOND THE DOJO

Paying attention isn't just being on the lookout for bad guys. In fact, if all you're doing is looking for bad guys, you're missing a lot. In other words, you're not paying attention very well at all!

Paying attention means being aware. Being present. It's what we practice in meditation and take to all areas of our training—and beyond our training.

I see so many people fail to pay attention, especially when driving. When you're driving, your goal is to reach your destination—safely! But I see so many people texting when they're in the car or focusing on something else, like eating a sandwich. There's such a lack of engagement here. Are they texting? Are they eating? Or are they actually driving?

If you're not paying attention, and if you're not engaged, guess what? You're not in control. That's why there are so many accidents when people text and drive. If you're a martial artist, you're a martial artist everywhere. Pay attention. Be engaged. Maintain control.

FOR THE PARENTS

A lot of parents have an awareness of their kids' surroundings and situations, but they don't know how to change them if they're unhappy with them.

For example, everyone knows that most kids today spend too much time watching TV or being on the computer. The majority of the time, technology isn't teaching kids anything productive. However, a lot of parents struggle to stop their kids from doing it. They don't feel like they can create new surroundings.

Growing up, I remember my house was full of arguments. My parents often yelled at me and my siblings. For example, if we weren't doing well at school, they would yell at us. I hated arguing then, and I still hate it now. These days, I avoid arguments in my house as much as possible.

Remember that children choose their role models based on what they watch and the people they spend time with. A kid's surroundings either inspire them or affect them in a negative way.

Pay attention to your child's behavior. If you notice a change in their behavior, don't be afraid to start a calm conversation with them. When it comes down to it, you want your child to have positive inspirations. In other words, once you've paid attention to what they're doing—*really* paid attention—have a conversation about it. Don't yell and scold. Ask them about what they are doing on the tablet. Maybe it's a game you'll like, too! They might just be spending too much time doing it. If you're having that conversation, you're engaged.

If you're paying attention and engaged, you're in a much better position to be in control. But unlike self-defense, you don't have to be fighting.

CHAPTER 8

✳ ✳ ✳

SPAR

LESSON: CONTROL
RULE: CONTROL
GOAL: CONTROL

In sparring, the goal, rule, and lesson are all the same. Sparring is all about control. It's simple. In sparring, your goal is to hold control, no matter the situation or how hard your partner hits you. The rule is to have control of yourself.

Everybody teaches different lessons about sparring. When I practice sparring with students, I make them think of it as a game of tag. To win the game, they must tag the other person a certain number of times (I think of a new number every time, just to keep it fun). Because sparring is a game, we can create the habit of staying positive. We get used to having this attitude, just like muscle memory.

When you're training, it's important to have an ultimate goal. In sparring, your ultimate goal should be to have control. (In my experience is it's easier to be angry than to have control, which is exactly the reason we try so hard to practice control.) To reach that ultimate goal, you have to practice reaching certain mini goals—just like the benchmarks we set in stretching. For example, tagging your partner once is a smaller goal which will ultimately help you develop control. By just focusing on each individual tag, you're present in the moment instead of being lost in the future.

WHAT SPARRING TEACHES
SELF-CONTROL

When someone hits you, your instinct usually tells you to hit them back harder. Think of any time you see two people start shoving each other on the playground. But in that situation, does anyone really have control?

In sparring, you can control the outcome by inspiring your partner.

A motto in jiu-jitsu is to protect your strength. The martial arts are all very similar, and any fight is a game of chess, not a game of strength. By keeping a cool head and a positive attitude you can outmaneuver your opponent while maintaining your strength and your control.

If your opponent doesn't have this skill, they're going to get frustrated, try to go harder, and wear themselves out.

CONTROL OVER OPPONENT

If you can't control your opponent, you can't touch your opponent. If you can't control yourself, you can't control your opponent. If you can't control either yourself or your opponent, how do you expect to control your outcome?

To control our opponent, we must revisit the idea of awareness. We need to get a feel for our opponent. Are they quick on their feet? Are the slow, but strong? Do they seem to favor punching over kicking? Simple questions, but it's amazing how many people fail to ask them.

Think about it—every time you get into your car, you run through a similar sort of mental checklist. It might happen subconsciously, but you check that you have your keys, you fix your mirror and you make sure your windshield wipers are in place. That's what you need to do in order to control your opponent. Make that checklist second nature. If you don't know what you're fighting, how could you ever hope to control it?

CONTROL TO THE END

I see a lot of people play the victim when sparring.

Picture yourself practicing jiu-jitsu. Your partner submits you. You can control yourself by tapping out, or you can keep wrestling your partner and end up getting your arm broken. If you get hurt, you might feel an urge to blame your partner. But it's not your partner's fault if you're the one who lost control.

The great thing about sparring is that, unlike self-defense, it's practice. We can practice keeping our control all the way, even if we lose. If you can control yourself, your emotions, and your composure—even when getting tapped out or tagged by a punch—then you've mastered control.

HOW TO SPAR

The first step in sparring is communication. Sparring can mean a lot of things. You might be working in a certain position or with a limited number of moves. You may be sparring light, or your partner may want to spar with a lot of intensity. If that's the case, you're going to want to know!

Sometimes people don't talk about how hard to hit or how intense to be. I'm not sure why, but I do know it's vital to make sure you're on the same page with your partner when it's time to spar. When you're not, that's when people get hurt (and even if no one gets hurt, no one is learning as well as they should be.)

Sparring is the same thing as playing a sport. You have to be safe and use the right equipment for whatever kind of sparring you're doing.

TIPS FOR SPARRING

So how do we keep this control? How do we become good partners and improve our technique through sparring? Let's look at some ways to do it.

MAKE YOUR OWN SPAGHETTI

In my gym we usually practice sparring on Wednesdays. On Wednesdays, our parents make spaghetti for dinner.

There are hundreds of combinations for spaghetti dishes. You can mix in meatballs or tomato sauce. It can be vegetarian.

When my wife makes spaghetti, she puts the water on and waits for it to boil, then she throws in the spaghetti, drains it, and adds a bunch of ingredients before eating it in a big bowl with cheese. I'm Asian, so I make spaghetti a little differently. For example, I don't wait for the water to boil before throwing the spaghetti in. It's all in the pan from the start. My spaghetti and my wife's spaghetti are completely different.

Just like spaghetti, sparring is about combination. When you're sparring, what kind of combination do you want to do? How are you going to go through it? What techniques are you going to use, and how are you going to use them? The basics don't change—spaghetti is still noodles and sauce—but how you choose to make yours is up to you.

Be creative. Be unique.

FOLLOW THE RULES

I know a lot of people who get nervous when sparring because they don't know the rules. The problem isn't that they don't know, it's that they don't ask! They're scared of sparring because they lack a clear idea of the lesson and goal.

Whatever your goal in life, you have to learn the lessons and know the rules to get there.

When you're driving, a red light means stop. That's a rule. If a driver runs the light, they've broken that rule and are dangerous to others. They're out of control. As a driver, the stoplight controls you. You have to follow that rule.

It's the same with sparring. For example, there's a reason I call the sparring game "tag." We're not trying to knock each other out in sparring, because that's an unsafe way to train. My students know to stop when I say stop. If they don't, their partners might relax, put their hands down, get punched when they're not expecting it and get hurt.

Respect the rules.

BE SAFE

Sparring is designed to be fun, and it is. As long as you spar safely.

For example, say your partner's hand is down. The timer hasn't gone off, they're still sparring, they're just not doing a great job. Instead of pounding them, you can just give them a light tag. Maybe even tag the hand that's down or gently tap one of their legs they're leaving too still. Instead of hurting them, you can say something like, "you left your leg there" to remind them. Now you're being safe, and you're being a good partner, and you're improving your technique. You're safe because no one got hurt. You're a good partner because you just helped them learn better technique. And you're improving because you still got the tag without having to punch your hardest—you proved that you could spot a mistake and capitalize on it.

All that, and you were safe the entire time. There's no need for us to try and kill each other while sparring. That's called being responsible.

ENJOY THE CHALLENGE

Not only is sparring supposed to be fun, it's supposed to be challenging.

When you win a fight, never forget your opponent. Why? Your opponent is the reason you became a champion. Without your opponent, you wouldn't have been able to win.

If an opponent gives you a good fight when sparring, treasure that. In sparring, winning and losing doesn't matter. It's about stepping up and embracing the challenge. You'll feel a much greater sense of achievement and satisfaction if you approach it that way instead of worrying about who's better.

EMPOWER OTHERS

If your opponent fails to challenge you, sparring won't feel like a game anymore.

So don't be that partner.

Empower others by challenging them.

Imagine your partner reaches their hand out, and you tag it. The second time, they don't keep their hand in the same place. Instead, they make you work for it. That approach is much more likely to inspire you. You're both learning in this situation, both growing, both empowering each other to try harder.

A SPARRING STORY

I once had a member of staff who was a very angry person. I could tell, because at one time, I was the exact same way. Unfortunately, he didn't learn the same lessons I did, and in time I ended up letting him go.

When he worked for me, he would come into the gym and act cool because he cared what everyone thought about him. But on the inside he was angry. He wasn't grateful for what he had in his life. Perhaps he had a rough life, but unfortunately he didn't seek or accept the support he had available to him in the dojo. During sparring one day, he got punched in the head. He had his hands down. It was his fault.

Was he a gracious sparring partner? Was he thankful that he'd found a hole in his technique to improve? No. He ran outside and screamed a profanity.

"Wow, you were very angry," I told him when he came back into the gym. He tried to deny it. I reminded him what angry looked like, but he told me he wasn't angry. I said he could deny it all he wanted, but the camera could see his anger.

Then I pulled up the video of him running outside on the security camera and played it for him. I even muted the sound and we watched the video footage again. I asked him if he thought he looked angry or happy. He didn't say anything. He just walked away.

At that point, there was nothing I could do. Some people just can't accept who they are. They know the difference between right and wrong, but they struggle to be honest. Not with anyone else, but with themselves.

When we spar, we can't avoid the honesty. All we can do is accept it or run away.

Don't run away from the truth.

BEYOND THE DOJO

Let's say you're driving on the highway and someone cuts you off. Is it worth it to get angry? That's the typical response, but for a true martial artist, it's not an option.

The awareness we practice in sparring transcends the dojo because it teaches us to remain calm in stressful situations, on and off the mat.

Sparring isn't about winning. It isn't about beating

another person. It's about knowing you can handle yourself and be present in a tough situation.

Just as you would not get angry in sparring if someone tags you, you shouldn't get angry if someone cuts you off in traffic. Or, if you are angry, you don't let the anger control you. In sparring, you learn to be calm and respond appropriately to keep yourself safe. The same is true in life, whether that's with your family, driving on the highway, anywhere.

If you're not aware someone cut you off, you might react emotionally instead of intelligently responding. If it's your mistake, you can get past your own ego and acknowledge it. You can take responsibility if it's your mistake. If it's their mistake, you can be thankful that you were aware enough, and good at sparring enough, to respond in a calm way that kept everyone on the road safe.

FOR THE PARENTS

When I ask my kids to do me a favor and help clean the house, their response isn't always positive. If they refuse, I tell them they have two choices. Their first choice is to be responsible and support me so that I can support them in return. For example, when they finish helping me clean, they can ask me for a favor in return.

Their second choice is to refuse my request and not help me clean. However, in that case, they will face some consequences.

As a parent, I need to adapt in such situations. Either I can get angry and start an argument, or I can communicate with my children in a calm way. I call this verbal sparring. That way, I will hopefully inspire my children the same way I'd inspire an opponent in sparring.

Whenever you talk to your kid, make an effort to recognize their situation and surroundings. What kind of situation are they in right now? What's their mental state? For example, say your kid is in the living room watching TV. In that situation, there are a couple of things you need to do to connect with your kid. Remember, sparring is all about engagement. If you're not engaged with your child, you're not in control.

Always remember to be honest with your child. If you've had the worst day at work, it would be wrong to come home and take that frustration out on your child. Your kid isn't to blame if you've had a bad day at work. Instead, tell them you had a bad day at work, and ask about their day. Share together. Be good partners. If you're good partners, then when it's time to spar, you'll be good sparring partners.

Aug 1, 2019

 A gift for you

Hi Mom & Dad, This is the book the
kids Karate master wrote. He likens the
lessons from Karate with those of life.
Hope you enjoy, love, Sue

CHAPTER 9

✳ ✳ ✳

FEEDBACK

LESSON: LISTENING
RULE: MAKE EYE CONTACT
GOAL: BE ENCOURAGING, NOT NEGATIVE

In my gym, it doesn't matter if we work on self-defense, sparring, or pad-work. At the end of every class, we give feedback. We make a real effort to emphasize this feedback. Unfortunately, people don't always listen when others are talking to them. As a result, they don't take advice that could help them grow.

When you give and receive feedback, you should be in the neutral stance. This is similar to the attention stance. In the neutral stance, your feet are shoulder distance apart. You can either keep your hands by your side or have them behind your back. When you receive feedback, make sure you look your partner straight in the eye. Listen to them.

Acknowledge what they're saying without saying anything in response.

Say someone is giving you feedback, and you're moving your body or looking down. Chances are you're distracted and not really listening. If you don't listen to feedback, how are you going to understand what you need to work on?

WHAT FEEDBACK TEACHES

In my gym, my students either do an okay job, a good job, or an awesome job.

When I came to the US all those years ago, I remember my teacher never used the word "correct." No job I did was ever "good." Instead, everything I did was either "not correct" or "not good." As you can imagine, that made me feel horrible about myself.

In my opinion, every teacher has a responsibility to acknowledge their student's skills, whatever they may be.

Say you've never run before. One day you challenge yourself and are able to run one mile. You consider that an awesome job. On the other hand, a person who's run a half marathon would probably consider that an "okay" job.

It's important to remember that everyone has a different level of fitness and ability.

As a teacher, my first job is to acknowledge my students' level of fitness. My second job is to show them what's possible. I want to inspire you to reach that next level for yourself. Getting feedback is a lot like identifying those benchmarks we talked about in the stretching chapter. You improve bit by bit, not all at once.

THE IMPORTANCE OF LISTENING

When you ask someone a question during a conversation, it goes without saying that you should listen to their answer. You continue your conversation based on the answer they give you. This way, two people can keep each other in check and be on the same page when they're talking.

Unfortunately, we don't always do that.

The purpose of feedback is for you to understand yourself, where you are, and what you need to be doing better next time. Feedback helps you to recognize your strengths and areas in which you can improve. But you can't always evaluate all that on your own. You need to pay attention to what others have to say. You need to truly listen.

EYE CONTACT

Being a good listener means making eye contact. Don't just stare at the ground and nod like you already know what your partner or teacher is telling you. Look them in the eye. Show them you're listening. Not only will eye contact help you listen, it will also help you prove to your partners and your teachers that you know how to listen. You'll also be setting an example for your fellow students.

BEING ENCOURAGING

Giving feedback is part of being a martial artist. And even when we participate in critiques, we can be encouraging.

Every mistake is a chance to grow! Instead of focusing on what your partner did wrong, show them a way they can do it even better. Remember, there's no bad job. Did they do good, great, or awesome? Let them know and help them grow.

HOW TO GIVE FEEDBACK

Joe Hyams once said, "A dojo is an arena of the confined conflict where we confront an opponent who is not the opponent, but rather a partner engaged in helping us understand ourselves more fully." Often the lessons you learn in the dojo are not about physical movement. Sometimes the person standing in front of you is teaching you a lesson about who you are.

HAVE GOALS

I meet a lot of people who come to my gym without knowing their goal. They might be at the gym, but they totally lack a sense of purpose. They make no effort to check where they are. People in this position tend to hit a plateau at the end of their workouts and they don't understand why.

If you find yourself hitting a plateau, it's important to ask yourself why. The more you understand *why* you're in a situation, the more you can understand where you need to go. Ask yourself: Do you want to focus on better technique? Do you want to have better alignment in your body? Do you want to learn to be present in a certain moment?

When you know these things, you won't just have feedback, but also a goal to apply that feedback to.

LET OTHERS SUPPORT YOU

A lot of people are great at supporting others, but they're not great at asking for support themselves. Sometimes they're embarrassed to get feedback. Sometimes their egos are too big. But the reality is, the people around them often just want to be helpful.

Seek out and welcome others' support. That's what a dojo is for.

SOMETIMES YOU HAVE TO SURRENDER

You and I are training together. Throughout the exercise, I try to attack you, but you have a great defense, and I get frustrated. I have two choices: I can remain frustrated, or I can surrender to the truth of the situation and ask for feedback.

We need feedback even when we don't want it. Sometimes we just want to keep trying and trying—to figure it all out ourselves.

If I do that, and I still can't tag you while I'm sparring, I'm just wasting my time. However, if I stop and ask you what I'm doing wrong, and you show me something I can do to spar better, then I can grow. You can grow, too, because I'm posing a bigger challenge.

To make all this happen, however, I had to surrender to the truth of what I didn't know.

ACKNOWLEDGE INTIMACY

In my culture, we don't have a lot of intimacy. The most we do to show affection is to bow or shake hands.

As a martial artist, I see a hug as an intimate surrender of acceptance.

You see a lot of hugging in dojos, and that's because martial arts becomes an intimate thing. We're learning to fight each other. We're exposed. People see our mistakes. We point out each other's mistakes and help each other grow and challenge each other.

That creates a special kind of bond.

Support isn't always easy to find in life. That's part of what makes a dojo so special. Whenever anyone supports you, make sure to acknowledge that. Be mindful of the support you receive, whether that comes from your parents, teachers, or friends.

After class, I encourage my students to say thank you to whoever supports them. I also encourage them to offer a hug to the people who brought them to the gym, whether that's their parents or grandparents. A hug is a beautiful example of a connection between two human beings.

FIND THE PROOF

If I'm going to inspire someone to become better, I need to present them with evidence. That's why I carry out demonstrations in my gym. I want my students to see examples to recognize the difference between a good job and an awesome job.

It's not enough to say, "You could be punching better." You need to be able to provide the exact evidence to your partner—and you should seek that evidence from your partner when receiving feedback. *How* could a punch be better? Could you have rotated your hips more? Were you looking at the ground and not the target?

Those are the details that will help you improve.

DISCOVER YOUR ROUTE

I don't think in terms of right and wrong. For example, there are probably a lot of things wrong with the way I speak and communicate, as English isn't my first language. However, I'd never want the language barrier to stop me from inspiring others.

In my gym, there's no discrimination. For example, say a parent comes to me and says their kid has special needs. That doesn't discourage me from training them. Instead, it motivates me. I make it my goal to find ways to communicate with that kid. That kid might just need to find his own route to "awesome" that will be different from some other kids' routes.

The same is true for all of us. Think of it this way: While your house is always going to be in the same spot, there are different routes you can take to get there. You've probably memorized the fastest way—but that's the fastest way for *you*. For your brother, or sister, or mom, or dad coming home from work, they have to take a different route. The goal of getting home doesn't change, but *how* each of you accomplishes it can.

The same is true in martial arts. We all have similar goals of mastering our art and winning competitions. But how each of us reaches that goal is a path we have to find.

EXPRESS GRATITUDE

Whenever someone offers you feedback, be grateful for it. Remember that the purpose of feedback is to help you learn and improve. By offering you feedback, your partner keeps you in check. They remind you of the things it's important to know.

Say your hand is down. Instead of hurting you, your partner gives you a reminder by tapping you. That's an easy lesson.

If your partner taps your hand to remind you, you should be grateful for that. It shows they care about you. They want to give you feedback to help you learn. The next day, when you come in and spar again, you'll remember that you're supposed to put your hands up.

A true partner will tell you what you need to work on. Be grateful for that. Tell them thank you.

A FEEDBACK STORY

If you don't want someone to see your behind, don't climb high.

Years ago, I was at a training session where we were told to climb to the top of an electric pole. At the top, we had to stand on a circular disk. Basically, the idea was to stand at the top of that plate and everyone else would spin you.

At that training, a lot of people were nervous to climb the pole. Not because they were scared of heights, but because they didn't want the people at the bottom to see their behinds. One lady wanted to be up at the top of the pole, but she didn't want to climb up there. In her eyes, she was too fat, and she was afraid of being judged for that.

In reality, every person who climbed to the top was given a round of applause by everyone below.

Nowadays, people are literally scared to achieve success. Either they're worried about someone looking at their behind, or they're afraid of being judged by others.

If you're that person, here's a question for you. What's your goal? What is it that you actually want to achieve?

The woman I mentioned above took the time to work on herself. She listened to the feedback she received from her training partners, and she kept improving herself. And eventually she did the thing she never thought she could do and climbed the pole.

BEYOND THE DOJO

In the gym, feedback is pretty obvious. If I see you can improve your punch, it's easy for me to walk over to you and help you improve. In real life, sometimes feedback isn't as obvious.

Let's say you got a bad grade on your homework or a test. It's easy to get angry about that, but you shouldn't. That's feedback.

A lot of times I hear students complain about their teachers. They think their teachers are mean or just hate them. But what they should really be feeling is grateful. Every time you get a grade, that's feedback. That's a way for you to know how to grow and be smarter.

You have a choice—one that should sound familiar by this point in the book. You can do the right thing, or you can play the victim. A victim thinks the teacher is out to get him. A martial artist sees a grade as feedback, recognizes his mistakes, and takes action.

FOR THE PARENTS

Let me tell you about my daughter. She's about to turn ten years old. She's very outgoing. She's been learning martial arts since she was very young, and has grown up competing and being around inspiring people, and it's given her an incredible spirit. Despite all that, there are still times when she tells me she's going to do something, but then she doesn't do it. As a parent, it's my job to explain to her that she and I have to respect one another.

"Do you want to keep the same respect or do you want to lose respect?"

When I ask a question like that, I'm opening up a couple of possibilities and giving my daughter a choice. If I tell her to do something and she chooses not to listen, then I explain that if she chooses not to respect me, there will be consequences. For example, if she doesn't clean her room now, she still has to clean it later. If she does it later, she might lose time doing other things that she wants to do.

As a parent, situations like this don't always feel good. Sometimes I feel I'm being harsh. However, it's my responsibility to explain things to my daughter so that she fully understands. I have to give the proper feedback.

Sometimes it's easy for parents to forget they have to make certain sacrifices for their children. Sometimes parents have to surrender.

Whatever you say, be honest with your kids. Sometimes parents forget how old their kids are or the environment they're in.

CHAPTER 10

✳ ✳ ✳

PICK UP A WEAPON

LESSON: DISCIPLINE
RULE: FINISH WHAT YOU BEGIN
GOAL: SYNCHRONIZE YOUR ACTIONS

I meet a lot of parents who want their kids to be in a weapons class. But not all kids are ready. At my gym, you must be invited into the weapons class. It's a class for those who are seeking greatness, but you have to be ready to seek greatness. Students need to demonstrate certain qualities in order to be invited.

WHAT WEAPONS TEACH US

In a weapons class, there are new lessons to be learned.

But it is also a class for those who have shown they've already learned certain important lessons.

DISCIPLINE

If they want to be invited, the number one thing students must demonstrate—and continue to demonstrate—is discipline. Weapons can be dangerous, and that's why discipline is so important.

Also, in a weapons class, we don't teach more than one technique at a time. When taught a new technique, students must practice it over and over until they've perfected it. That requires a lot of discipline.

FINISHING WHAT YOU BEGIN

Discipline means following through. If I invite you into my weapons class, that means I believe you're already the type who will follow through on your intentions. It means you have already proven that you can.

In a weapons class, it's more important than ever to finish what you start. Once you own a weapon, you possess something that is dangerous in untrained hands. If I invite you to learn to use a weapon, I expect you to train with discipline until you have mastered using it.

SYNCHRONIZING YOUR ACTIONS

If a student is using a weapon and they're not focused, they risk injury—either to themselves or to a classmate. I don't allow that kind of chaos in my weapons class. We must be disciplined and committed enough that we can train in a safe and synchronized way.

HOW TO TRAIN WITH WEAPONS

The first step in weapons training is choosing the weapon for you.

We train with five weapons at my dojo: the tonfa, nunchaku, staff, sai, and sword.

As we'll see later in this chapter, each of these weapons has its own characteristics, its own personality, if you will. And they will also take on the personality that you bring to them.

Choosing your weapon is important because the weapon is a reflection and extension of you. People often pick up weapons thinking that they are in control of the weapon when, in fact, it is a partnership. When you train with a weapon, you learn to control it by being with the weapon.

For example, I love the sword. The sword is sharp. It reflects the sharpness of my tongue. One fundamental principle in sword training is that you don't want to make any more cuts than necessary. You cannot swing wildly and try to win with a thousand cuts. The goal is one swift, accurate cut.

Similar to my tongue, if I let it work its danger carelessly it will reflect on me poorly. If someone yells at me, it is important that I know how to use my weapon and be as direct and honest in my words as I can.

Once we have our weapon, the first lesson is safety. We learn to take the weapon from its place and how to return it. We learn to respect the weapon and what it is capable of.

TIPS FOR WEAPONS TRAINING

So how do we cultivate this discipline, commitment, and synchronization?

When it comes to weapons, there are lots of things to learn and remember along the way. Let's look at what else we should know as we prepare for weapons training.

CHOOSE YOUR WEAPON WISELY

It all starts with choosing your weapon.

Your weapon is an extension of you, and therefore it

should reflect who you are and how you train. In my classes, I bring out all the weapons and let my students choose which one speaks to them. I tell them to trust their heart. First, the kids close their eyes. Then they open their eyes and pick up the weapon that speaks to their heart.

Every weapon has its own personality, and identity, and character. They're all good at something different. For example, a sword can cut, but you can't use it to carry things. With a bo, you can whip it, spin it—and carry things. Using a bo, you can hit hard or soft. The bo can also be used as a defense mechanism. If someone hits you hard, you can use the bo to defend the hit. The nunchaku flow and can capture weapons, whereas the tonfa, even though it can lash out and strike the nunchaku, is stiff and deflects. The sais have the ability to capture and have the sharpness of the sword, but are more compact and do not have the reach of the bo or sword.

Each has sharpness, strength, and flexibility. It depends on how you use it.

The nunchaku, for example, is a slow weapon. Although it can hit hard, you have to hit in slow motion because of how the weapon is built. A nunchaku has a rope or chain in the middle, which makes it difficult to use for blocking. Instead, you have to use flow motions to catch the weapon. Does that resonate with you? Perhaps you're not the fastest, but you know you move fluidly and can hit hard. The nunchaku, then, might be the weapon for you.

Even though each weapon has its own function, the technique is similar. For example, you hit a stick and a sword in the same direction. Similarly, you can take the bo and stab forward. If you know how to throw a punch, you can use a weapon. The difference is the increased responsibility and the need for discipline in your training.

REMEMBER THAT ALIGNMENT

Whenever you deliver a technique with a weapon, your body must be aligned with that weapon. Think of it like riding a bike. When you were learning to ride a bike, you probably thought that you controlled the bike. In reality, the bike controlled you. You were just the one *guiding* it. It was your job to make sure the bike went straight or took a turn, but ultimately the bike had the most power.

To ride well, you must be in complete alignment with your bike.

It's the same with a weapon. The weapon has a job to do, but it needs you in order to perform it. You must have alignment with yourself and your weapon to use that weapon well. Just as when you became good at riding a bike, and the bike felt like an extension of you, so it should be with your weapon.

STAY HUMBLE

When you choose to pick up a weapon, you have to pay attention to that weapon.

I see some kids come into a weapons class and try to show off in front of others. They get cocky and end up getting hurt.

My advice is to stay humble. You can put as much time and effort as you want into perfecting a skill, but you must remain humble throughout. When you get overconfident you take too many risks. And that's when you or someone else gets hurt.

STAY AWARE

Imagine fifteen students in a weapons class, all wielding different dangerous weapons.

You better stay aware of yourself and your surroundings.

Everyone should be aware.

This is another area where our previous lessons come into

play. In meditation, in stretching, and in our basics and sparring, we have learned awareness. Now we're taking it to the next level. We're using dangerous weapons. Our awareness is now a matter of safety.

ATTITUDE COMES FIRST

In a lot of martial arts schools, you have to reach a certain rank to be invited to a weapons class. I teach the opposite of that. In my eyes, if you listen at home, come to the gym consistently (three days a week), and your parents say you're behaving well, I'll invite you to weapons class.

Some kids train really hard in the gym, but then treat their parents badly at home. If that's the case, I won't invite that kid to weapons class. I go for the kids who might not have the best technique, but who listen at home. For me, these are the kids that show real potential. I can fix a student's technique. It's much harder to fix a student's attitude.

A WEAPONS STORY

I once had a student who was really good with weapons—particularly swords. But one time, when she was at a tournament, she was fooling around with a practice sword and dropped it. The sword sliced her foot open, and she started bleeding. The cut wasn't life-threatening, but it was bad enough that she could no longer compete in the tournament. In addition to the disappointment, she (or her parents) lost all the money they'd paid for her to compete. All of this was due to her losing her discipline and becoming unsynchronized.

BEYOND THE DOJO

Throughout history, martial artists have learned to use weapons to defend themselves.

In real life, you already have a weapon. You have two hands and two feet. But the most important weapon you have is your mouth. If anyone wrongs you, you should stand up for yourself by speaking up. However, there are also times when it is definitely *not* the time to use this weapon.

Often, we tend to use this weapon backwards. I know a lot of kids who talk back to their parents, but don't actually know how to stand up for themselves. In today's society, bullying has become a big problem, and kids not knowing how to defend themselves is a big part of the problem.

Kids often use their mouths to say negative things. In the dojo, I always tell kids that they can be as loud as they want, as long as they're being positive. If they want to yell, they have to yell positive words.

Words are your weapons outside the dojo. You can choose how to use your words. If you tell your parents you're going to clean your room, are you actually going to execute that? Are you going to live up to your word? How are you going to use your words to inspire? How are you going to become better? Are you disciplined and committed?

FOR THE PARENTS

If a student trains only at the gym, that's a good job, but not a great job. It's definitely not an awesome job.

Students do an awesome job if they go to the gym, train every single day, and then practice their skills outside the gym. This way, not only are they working on consistency and discipline, but they're also showing they care for themselves. They're showing their skills go beyond the dojo. They're living the life of a martial artist. That's what I call awesome.

Whether they want to do a good, great, or awesome job is up to my students. But often children don't know what they need to do an awesome job.

They need to be led. They need to be inspired.

If you are a parent, teacher, or instructor, your job is to lead and inspire your kids.

You have the same weapons as your kids—your words. It's up to you to choose whether you want to train yourself to do a good, great, or awesome job with them.

A lot of parents struggle with this. Instead of using their weapons to inspire when their kid does something they don't want, they use their weapons to put down, to scold, or to yell. And when the kid does a good job, parents often say nothing or, worse, ask something such as, "That's all you can do?"

As a parent, you have to make an effort to understand your child's situation. Instead of bringing them down, encourage them. Your weapons—your words—are more powerful than you imagine. Even when it seems they're not listening, your kids are listening. The way you use your words and react to your kid will affect how your kid looks at you. Ask yourself: How do you want them to see you?

The answer to that question is your goal. And if you can discipline yourself, commit to that goal, and synchronize yourself with those powerful weapons—your words—you can accomplish it.

CHAPTER 11

✳ ✳ ✳

COMPETING

LESSON: STRIVE TO BE BETTER
RULE: ASK QUESTIONS
GOAL: RECOGNIZE THE WIN

If you want to compare your skills to others, enter into a competition.

Students are often scared to enter competitions. Strange as it sounds, one of the best ways to get over your fear of competing is to—compete!

Think about the first time you took a new class or did an activity for the first time. Did you feel uncomfortable? I'm guessing the answer is yes. Maybe you felt scared, overwhelmed, anxious, or all of the above. Now think about how that feeling disappeared over time.

You can do this with competition as well. Even if you don't feel like it right now, take it from me: you can be a competitor.

WHAT COMPETITION TEACHES

STRIVING TO BE BETTER

Competing shouldn't just be about beating someone else. Every person you meet in life teaches you a lesson. The question is: how do you want to value that lesson?

That's the true purpose of competition. Sure, it's nice to win. And of course you always compete to win! But the point of competing to win is to learn where you are and what you need to do to grow. If you don't compete at your best, you'll never know where you still need to grow.

Don't just compete to win. Compete to grow. Strive to do your best, and then make your best better.

ASKING QUESTIONS

A big part of how you compete depends on how you ask for support.

Remember the chapter on feedback? Feedback is now more important than ever! Now is the time to understand your strengths and weaknesses so you know what you need to train.

If you've never competed before, this is also the time to ask for support mentally and emotionally. Stepping onto the competition mat can be intimidating. When you're practicing in a small arena, you have fewer spectators. In a big arena, there are so many more eyes on you. Often, this can seem scary.

Ask for support from your coach and teammates who have competed before. Ask them how they've dealt with the nerves, the butterflies, the distractions. Whatever you're worried about, trust me—someone else in your dojo has dealt with it. And if you're training in a good dojo, that person will be there to help you.

RECOGNIZING THE WIN

Imagine someone who comes into the gym every day. They put a lot of hard work in. They ask for support from others. From the outside, it looks like they're doing everything right. But what they might lack is a winning attitude.

In a competition, you win the experience. You win friendship. You win confidence and courage. There are so many different ways to win—far more ways than just winning medals and trophies.

Obviously, it feels good to win a trophy. It's a great reminder of your accomplishments. However, I've discovered that I learn a lot more when I lose.

When I lose a competition, I'm motivated to train harder. If I win, I usually take a couple of days off. When I lose, my mind is racing. I'm thinking of all the ways I can train even harder and become better than the opponent who beat me.

Having a Winning Attitude

When people lose, they have a tendency to get angry. Because of this attitude, they might talk back to their opponent or talk badly about them.

Winners don't always display the best attitude, either. I see a lot of winners who treat their opponents like trash. Winning gives them a sense of superiority. They think they're better than everyone around them. Is that really a winning attitude? In my opinion, that's not how a champion should act. It's not how a true martial artist should act.

I've met a lot of champions—true champions. The one thing all champions have in common is a great attitude. Instead of talking badly about their opponent, they shake hands. They spend time talking. They might even go out for dinner after a tournament. Often, people who have fought each other fiercely can end up the best of friends.

HOW TO COMPETE: MOVING FROM THE POND TO THE OCEAN

In the dojo, everyone knows everyone. Not only do we know each other, but we all train and spar with each other all the time. We know who is good at what and who is at what level. We know all of each other's best moves. Even though we can all help each other grow, it's healthy to test your skills against a totally unfamiliar opponent after a while.

The dojo, in other words, is a small pond. If you train every day and work to perfect your technique, you become the king of the small pond. That can feel good. *Too* good. You don't want to only be king of the small pond. Some people are too afraid to step outside their own dojos where they're king, and they never grow. The way to challenge yourself is to move out of that small pond. You have to test your skills in the ocean.

TIPS FOR COMPETING

Of course some of the biggest things you'll need to know for competition will come from your own coach and your own training. Still, there are some tips that can apply to anyone who's just getting started in competing.

COMMIT

It's a big commitment to sign up for a tournament. For one, it's not cheap to enter a tournament. One thing I recommend doing is paying to enter the tournament yourself. You might expect your parents to pay for it, and that can be okay, but you're much less likely to value yourself if somebody pays for you to participate in a tournament.

Even if your parents pay for you to compete, you have to understand what it truly means to sign that paper that says you're competing. You're bowing. You're choosing in.

You have to prepare. You have to ask for support.

BE NERVOUS

When I was younger, I lied to my dad before every competition. I'd tell him I wasn't nervous. I wanted to seem confident in front of him.

In reality, *everyone* gets nervous when they compete. It's normal to feel a sense of anxiety. When you experience those symptoms, recognize what you're feeling. Don't try to ignore them. That will only make it worse. Embrace them. Know it's normal. That's how you learn to become better.

EMBRACE THE STRUGGLE

You need to know how it feels to be challenged, both in the gym and in life. That's a big part of what competition is about. Perhaps you live a life where you don't have too many struggles. If so, competing is what you need. You need to test yourself and see what it is like to truly struggle.

Struggling helps develop empathy. If you know how it feels to struggle, you're in a better position to understand other people when they struggle.

CALCULATE YOUR TRAINING

After you sign up for a tournament, you need to plan how you'll prepare for that tournament. How many hours can you dedicate to training without putting too much pressure on yourself?

Even though you want to train enough, you also want to avoid overtraining. I see people all the time who train too much and end up injuring their bodies. Obviously, this isn't good for them, and it doesn't help them perform any better when they compete—if they can compete at all.

KNOW YOU CAN WIN

I hear people say that they don't think of themselves as

competitors. That's not true. If someone doesn't want to compete, the real reason is that they're afraid of losing.

I believe everyone has a competitive drive inside them.

Here's an example I use with my students. When a man sees a beautiful lady, he wants to get to know her. Now imagine he gets nervous and starts telling himself that the lady doesn't want to speak to him or that she has a boyfriend. That man buys into his own made-up story about why he shouldn't get to know the lady.

In reality, he's just afraid.

You're capable of doing anything that you want. It's just hard. It's a struggle to get what you want. That's why learning to struggle is so important. And why knowing that you can succeed is so important.

BE HUMBLE

Both winning and losing are reflections on your character. The people who maintain a great attitude remain on top. Others remain at the bottom. When it comes to attitude, medals and trophies don't mean anything.

Inevitably, winning can get to your head sometimes. When I was younger, I'd win a tournament, go back to the gym, and have a bad attitude around my teammates. At the next tournament, guess what would happen? I'd lose.

If you want to win, you have to carry a winning attitude every single day. As a mentor, parent, teacher, or instructor, you keep that humble mindset of a true winner. That's being a true martial artist.

A COMPETITION STORY

Let me share an example of someone who learned this lesson the hard way.

I trained a black belt student who once won a tournament. Naturally, he was incredibly happy about his win. The next day, when he came back into the gym, he didn't train. He didn't choose in. Instead of training that day, he sat around while everyone else jumped rope.

"You can't have that attitude toward winning," I told him.

"But I just won," he said.

I tried to explain that he won yesterday. Today is a totally new day.

Three months later, this student competed in another tournament. You guessed it, he lost. Instead of accepting his loss, he called his opponent "lucky." He tried to convince me of all the reasons the other guy beat him.

I said he could try and convince me all he wanted. In reality, he knew exactly what he did wrong. For three months following his win, he'd had the wrong attitude. The day he lost, my advice to him was to accept the loss and learn his lesson instead of trying to justify what had happened.

And he did. He kept quiet. The next time he came to the gym, he trained harder. He didn't wait for me to tell him to jump rope. He just did it. He realized what he had to do, so he put the extra work in.

BEYOND THE DOJO

In life, when things get hard, people are quick to throw in the towel and give up. When you lose in a tournament, that's an experience. Are you really going to give up your whole martial arts career because of one loss?

Losing in martial arts prepares us for the inevitable losses we'll face in life. We'll do badly on tests. We'll get dumped. We'll have bad days.

In the dojo, we practice getting back to work. In life, we can practice the same thing.

Tomorrow is a new day. It's another opportunity to get back into training. It's a chance to become better.

When something challenges you in life, you have to ask yourself: What's important? How can you pass that difficult point? How can you overcome that challenge? If you look at things the same way all the time, you won't see a different possibility for a different result. Any problem has a number of solutions, as long as you look hard enough. Just because you lost, that doesn't make you a loser.

A win always gets celebrated. While nobody really celebrates a loss, losses make us better. When you make a mistake in a relationship, and you work through that mistake, the relationship gets stronger. When I lost my business, I was more motivated than ever to work toward something better. I knew where I wanted to be, and I always knew where I *didn't* want to be. This constant reminder made me want to be better.

FOR THE PARENTS

How do you win as a parent?

It feels like we're losing or failing, all the time. Sometimes we are. What's important is to make sure that we learn from our losses.

Imagine your kid tells you he wants to play basketball (or sign up for martial arts). Maybe you think it sounds like a fine idea, but you realize you never actually signed him up, or you got busy and didn't take him to practice.

It's easy as parents to play the victim. We have jobs, bills, and responsibilities. Things get in the way. We let some things slide. We excuse ourselves when what we should do is take responsibility.

It's not that different from learning martial arts. Imagine yourself in a tournament. You keep trying your best kick, but you just can't hit your opponent. You lose. What do you do? You go back to the drawing board. You ask for support, and you support yourself by getting to the root of the problem. Perhaps you discover that it wasn't necessarily your kick that was bad, but your footwork. So you train your footwork. Now your kick is better. Now you're ready to succeed.

Look for the root problems in your parenting. Is driving your kids to where they need to be a problem? Okay. Ask yourself how you can solve that problem. Can you work out a carpool deal with another parent? Can you adjust your schedule? Is there work you could do while your kid is at practice, killing two birds with one stone?

We're great at finding problems in our parenting, but not so great at working at the solutions.

Compete. Lose. Learn. Win.

CHAPTER 12

✳ ✳ ✳

TESTING

LESSON: REVIEW

RULE: SHOW UP

GOAL: ADVANCE TO NEXT RANK

Just like competition, testing is a way of measuring what a student can do. It is also a way of determining whether a student advances in belt rank. At my gym, we usually announce a test about a month prior. It gives students a chance to review, reflect, and practice.

All schools do testing differently. At my gym, prior to a test, we create a chart. That helps kids see what they don't remember or identify what skills they don't yet have. If a student sees they lack something, they're more likely to ask for support. In my gym, we have a leadership team. When a kid needs some support, they ask the leadership team for advice. If they need extra practice, they can coordinate a time that works for their parents and the gym.

Like everything else, testing involves making a choice. I ask my students: Do you want to take initiative and pass the belt test? Or do you prefer to not take initiative and fail the test? I make sure they understand any result will be a reflection of their initiative and hard work.

ADVANCING TO THE NEXT RANK

In a testing situation, your goal is to get the next belt. A belt helps you recognize your level. It's a visual representation of your benchmark.

When I was training to be a martial artist, there were no ranks. Now, ranks have become quite commercial. Gyms are interested in making money, and belt tests can be a way to make money.

That doesn't take away from the fact that belts are a way to track your progress. If you're in a dojo with a coach who cares about you, it won't be about money. It will be about the honor and recognition of growing as a martial artist. They're a great visual. With belts, you know what your current rank is, and you know how you can advance to get to the next rank.

A belt increases your drive to want to improve. Would you be happy going to college if there was no graduation at the end of your degree? Belts are like degrees. They're a way to show you've kept growing.

WHAT TESTING TEACHES
REVIEWING

Now is the time to really think about where you are as a martial artist and what you have to study.

The word "test" instantly makes people anxious. Kids get anxiety because they assume that any test is difficult. When they hear talk of a test, they associate it with tests at school.

I don't want anyone to feel stressed about a test in martial arts. In my gym, I tell my students that there are three ranks (grades) they can get. The three levels are C, B, and A.

C stands for, "Come on, you can do better."

B stands for, "Best."

A is for "Awesome."

I deliberately make the grades more fun. The way I provide the information affects how my students feel about tests. When tests are more fun, reviewing results is more fun. And when students feel more positive, they learn and grow more.

SHOWING UP

Like the weapons class, not everyone gets to test for the next rank. I invite students to test based on the discipline they show in class. My students know this. If they get invited to a test, they know it is an honor.

There are a couple of things I need to see from my students in order to invite them to test. First, I need to see attendance. My students have to show up to class if they want to move forward and get better. But it's not enough to just show up to class. I also need to see my kids participating. I want them to be engaged and ask questions. I also test my kids' memory, discipline, and behavior, both inside and outside the gym.

HOW TO TEST

The biggest part of taking any test is preparation.

In my dojo, once you're invited to test, you have two weeks to prepare to review.

In the preparation class, they get all the answers they'll have for the test. We want the student to know what the test is about. We don't have a hidden agenda or want to trick them. We want to make sure that they are prepared.

We also want to know that they—and their parents—are committed. They get to practice in the dojo, but true commitment means they're learning at home. I tell them the more practice they get, the more committed they are because when they're doing it on their own, they're showing true dedication. They're showing self-discipline and determination. It's one thing when your sensei is telling you to do something in class. To do it on your own is something else.

TIPS FOR TESTING

It takes a lot of courage to show up to a test or a competition.

Even if you throw up after riding a roller coaster, you still had the courage to ride it in the first place. This is a personal example I use in my gym. I don't like roller coasters, but my kids love them. If I go on a roller coaster, I do it to spend time with my kids. That takes a lot of courage. The more courage I have, the more fun I can have with my kids. The outcome might be that I throw up at the end of the ride. But it doesn't matter, because my kids and I can laugh about it together.

In other words, I show up.

Even if you have a weakness, be proud of yourself for having the courage to show up.

REMEMBER YOUR GOAL

Recognize your weaknesses. Identify your fears. But make sure you still align to yourself and your goal.

As crazy as it sounds, people can actually forget why they're at a belt test. If someone is nervous and anxious, and they let those feelings get the best of them, the test becomes a blur, and they don't perform at their best.

It's important to go into the test remembering what your goal is. If you have that focus all the way through, the negative feelings won't rise to the top.

BE YOUR OWN HERO

Let me tell you about Ben. Ben is a kid in my gym who's very strong, but he used to get nervous for every test. As an instructor, it's my responsibility to spot which kids are nervous and support them.

One time, I asked Ben for his superhero name. "Superman," he said. I told him he would have his own superhero name. "You're Brilliant Ben," I told him. "B stands for brilliant. So this test should be easy for you."

When he heard this, Ben smiled. Within a couple of seconds, he forgot what he was nervous about.

REMEMBER THE BASICS

The test is slightly different for each person based on their current rank. For example, white belts do what white belts need to do because their skills are not as advanced. However, black belts have to go through white belt and blue belt material. Although their skill levels are different, black belt students still have to work on all the same basic components as white belt students.

The basics always matter.

A BELT TEST STORY

I teach a student who comes to class and struggles with paying attention. When he pays attention, his head shakes a little. He can't keep his head straight; that's how his body functions. Despite this, this kid is extremely dedicated, focused, and committed to training. The only challenge he faces is keeping himself focused.

Whenever this student goes into a test, he gives 100 percent effort. He's desperate to reach his end goal. He's five years old.

During tests, we give him a small board to break. In one test, I remember asking him what his goal was.

"To break a board," he said.

"How do you break a board?" I asked.

"Go through the board."

"What stance are you in?"

"Fighting stance."

"What does fighting stance teach you?"

"Commitment."

"When the board breaks, do you show your commitment or not?"

"I show commitment. That means I get my belt."

When I put the board in front of him, he tried once and

didn't break it. He tried again, and the board didn't break. I tried repeating and rephrasing some questions.

"What stance are you in?" I asked again.

"Fighting stance," he replied.

"What does that teach you?"

"Commitment."

"Based on your result, do you think you committed?"

"No, sir. I did not commit."

This is where the support came in. I didn't fail him. I coached him. I helped him become his best self.

I told him, "You can ask for support. What can I do to support you so you can successfully pass this rank test?"

"Can you help me by teaching me how to break?" he asked.

Of course, I said I'd teach him to break a board. But I also wanted to prove the importance of support. I told him that, in life, he'd probably have a couple of people supporting him. For example, his parents would support him.

However, because he was in the gym, everybody could offer him support. The boy's name was Braden.

I asked the rest of the class, "Can everyone clap their hands and say, 'Go Braden!'?"

They clapped. They chanted his name.

And boom! Braden broke the board.

"Did you commit?" I asked him.

"Yes, I committed," he replied.

"What did you feel after you committed?" I asked. "There are three As I want you to think about."

"Awesome," he said.

"Yes, that's one," I said. "Do you know the other two? If you don't, I'll give them to you." Braden didn't know. "A stands for accomplishment and A stands for achieve," I said. "Did you achieve?"

"Yes, sir. I achieved."

Conversations like this help remind kids what tests are actually for.

Now let me tell you about another kid in my gym. This kid is fourteen years old, and he was never focused when he came to class. Throughout training, he always thought he was the best in the gym.

In class, we stacked three thick boards for him. He'd always try and show off and prove he was better than everyone else. Guess what happened? He couldn't break the boards. According to him, the boards were too hard, and his hand hurt.

At that point, I turned to another kid who did manage to break the boards.

"How old are you?" I asked.

"Seven," he said.

"How did you break the boards?"

"With confidence, sir. I know I'm strong."

"Earlier when you didn't break the boards, did your hand hurt?"

"No, sir."

That's when I turned back to the older kid. I explained

the importance of being honest with himself. If he was honest with himself, I could support him in breaking the boards. If he couldn't be honest with himself, I couldn't support him. He replied that he would be honest because he wanted my support.

"Listen to my directions," I said. "I'll count one, two, three and then, you yell out and hit. If you go through the boards, the boards will break because of your strength."

He hit the boards. They didn't break. He tried again, but he couldn't break the boards. According to him, he couldn't break the boards because his hand hurt. I asked him to try switching hands.

"Are you committed?" I asked him.

"Yes, sir."

Sometimes I have to rephrase the way I speak to my students.

"I can teach you, but you have to follow my directions. If you don't follow directions, you cannot follow through. This is how you're going to break the boards." At that point, I gave him a demonstration. "Now, I'm going to grab a shield. I'm going to ask you to hit the shield."

When he hit the shield, I asked, "Did you hear that sound?"

"Yes, sir," he said.

"With that sound, you'll have no problem breaking the boards. Are you ready?"

"Yes, sir."

That time, he was successful. He broke through the boards.

There was something I wanted him to know straight away. I said, "I want you to acknowledge something. Everything in life is about listening to directions. If you want to accomplish something, you have to listen to directions."

This is something I make clear to all my students. I always remind them to never underestimate the value of listening to directions.

I ended by saying, "Based on what you just did, you now have confidence and strength. Thank you for being honest." I turned to the class. "Everybody, give him a hand."

The whole class gave him a clap and he went to sit down. I could tell he was proud of himself.

BEYOND THE DOJO

In life, there are a lot of tests. Often waking up in the morning is a test. There's no point in trying to avoid challenges, because you'll always encounter them. Instead, you have to prepare yourself for tests and strive to pass them.

Always ask yourself what's important. For example, say you have to wake up at 6:00 a.m. What can you do to prepare yourself for that? In my opinion, there's no such thing as a night person or a morning person. You can be any person you want, as long as you change your behavior or thinking. If you have to wake up at 6:00 a.m., you need to prepare for that before you go to bed.

Your actions are based on your reactions. Say you go out tonight. How will you feel tomorrow when you remember what you did yesterday? Going out tonight is sabotaging yourself from commitment tomorrow.

It's our responsibility to rank up in life. We might not wear a different belt, but we will know where we've grown—and where we still need to improve—if we face life with the same determination that we face belt tests.

FOR THE PARENTS

As parents, we're tested all the time. It's not too different from competition—it's okay to fail.

What I think parents need to learn most from belt testing, however, is not just that it's okay for them to fail, it's okay for their children to fail as well.

When your child fails, there's always a lesson for them to learn. This is necessary. Often I see parents who want to see their child get promoted even more than the kid does. Over and over, I see parents who are afraid to see their children fail.

Here's what you need to know: Your children, even though they must learn to try to win, must also learn to fail. They need to learn that failing is okay.

As a parent, instead of focusing on failure, focus on experience. Focus on the lesson to be learned. If your focus is there, then your child will learn that failure isn't the thing that she should be focusing on, but learning.

The place you're in today is because of the failures you've made in the past. People fail all the time, and then they get better. Share these experiences with your child.

Imagine a parent constantly reminding their kid of a mistake they made. That will be a negative experience for the kid. There's no lesson for them there, just a reminder they did something poorly. Alternatively, you could talk to and listen to your child. Ask yourself: Are you giving your child the support they need? Are you being patient with them?

Not every problem needs to be fixed immediately. Some problems just need to be acknowledged. Some parents care so much what others think of them that they try and fix their child right away.

Let them struggle. Love them through the struggle. Watch as they learn to fight their battles.

CHAPTER 13

✳ ✳ ✳

CHOOSING A MENTOR

LESSON: BE UNCOMFORTABLE
RULE: TAKE RISKS
GOAL: IMPROVE YOURSELF

In martial arts, it's important to have a mentor.

In life, there are different types of mentors. For example, when a kid's growing up, their parent is often their mentor. Parents have more life experience than their kids. Chances are they've made mistakes they can teach their kids to avoid.

But parents aren't the only mentors available. Personally, I've gotten to where I am today because of my martial arts teacher. Don't get me wrong—I'm grateful for my parents and I'm even more grateful that they brought me to martial arts all those years ago. But growing up, I saw my martial arts teacher as a second father.

Often people refuse to believe that they need a mentor. They think they can do everything on their own. Sure, there are things we can do on our own. As a businessman, I got to where I am without a business mentor. However, if I'd had someone to help me avoid certain things and teach me lessons I had to learn on my own the hard way, I may have found success sooner and spared myself some unnecessary grief.

This doesn't mean I won't ever need a business mentor. If I want to kick things up a notch, I need to find a mentor who's better at business than I. Someone who can guide me and teach me the secrets to improving my business.

We can all use mentors. Mentors push us to surpass them. And then, one day, we can become mentors and do the same thing for those we choose to help. In this way, our communities constantly grow.

WHAT MENTORS TEACH

Mentors can teach you anything—as long as you can find the right mentor.

Before you look for a mentor, there are two important points to consider. The first is whether you're willing to give up your time. The second is whether you're willing to pay. If you're not willing to invest money or time, you'll struggle to find a mentor.

When you find your mentor, don't expect things to be easy. Here are the three things you should expect to experience when you find your mentor.

BE UNCOMFORTABLE

A good mentor won't let you feel too comfortable.

Honesty can be harsh. But if you pay for a mentor, you're paying for honesty. Any successful, established mentor will want to help change you. Change is uncomfortable.

A mentor sees how great you can be because they've achieved greatness themselves. They also know this doesn't come easy.

You should expect to be uncomfortable because to become great you must go through adversity. Think of it like lifting weights. You only get stronger by pushing your muscles. Lifting weights is hard. It's easy to give up. But if you have someone there pushing you, convincing you that you can do it and giving you tips on how to do it, you're more likely to push through that discomfort and come out the other side stronger.

TAKE RISKS

A mentor can teach you confidence, commitment, trust, and determination, among so many other things.

They should also teach you to take risks.

A mentor might push you to compete and risk losing. A business mentor might push you to invest and risk losing money. Or risk losing face. People are often afraid to take risks because they fear losing face with their family and friends, and as a consequence, they lose trust in themselves. But there's no growth, no real evolution, without risk taking.

Risk taking, by its very nature, is scary. Just like with lifting weights, sometimes we need someone to prod us along and give encouragement to find the courage to take the necessary risks for growth.

Recognize that good things happen when you take risks. To this day, I can still be scared of sparring at times. However, I still take that risk constantly. It continues to pay off.

IMPROVE YOURSELF

Some people are so terrified to lose face that they don't think about improving themselves. Instead, they prefer to improve what other people see of them. For example, they might be struggling to pay their mortgage, but buy a new car to show off. For some people, it's all about face.

In reality, it doesn't matter what anyone else thinks of you. When you're dead, nobody thinks about you anyway. The older you get, the wiser you become and the less you care about what other people think.

The sooner you learn this lesson, the better.

Instead of focusing on strangers, focus on yourself and your family. How can you maintain your own honor and integrity? What's right for you?

HOW TO FIND A MENTOR

People, a lot of times, don't want help. Sometimes people see the word mentor and they think of it as someone who is telling you what to do. A mentor is not a weak thing.

Each one of us has skills, but we all lack certain skills.

There is so much information out there—at the library, or on the internet. You can also pay a mentor for their time.

A lot of people read *Rich Dad Poor Dad*, for example. It's a very popular book. Some people read the book and collect information. It's another thing to know how to apply that information and have expert guidance. Books are great, but they can't take you all the way. They can't support you.

No one is above having a mentor. Even I still have mentors, whether it's for writing a book or even martial arts. I need to keep training, and I need to keep growing to be a good leader.

Even if you have skills, you should always want to be better, and that's where mentors can help, because mentors challenge, push, and give feedback.

The way you find a mentor is simple: you ask.

That's the biggest obstacle, because people don't want to ask. They don't want to ask and they don't want to pay. People often have too much pride to ask, and don't have the determination to pay. People often say, "I don't have money for that," but they need to look at where they are and where they really want to go. And if they're not willing to pay for it, they shouldn't complain. It's rarely an issue of not being able to afford it. Usually, it's about being willing to spend the money on a mentor instead of something else.

Do you want to grow or decay? If you're fine with decaying, then don't complain. But if you want to grow, then what do you need to do? You need a mentor. And you need to do what it takes to get one. You have to ask, and you probably will have to pay.

TIPS FOR BEING MENTORED

Tips for being mentored? Isn't it the mentor's job to do the mentoring? Well, yes, but it's up to you to do the work. Here are some things to keep in mind as you seek out a mentor and once you find one.

IDENTIFY WHAT YOU NEED

When looking for a mentor, identify what you need. What kind of mentor are you looking for? Do you need help with your technique? Your attitude? Your competition mindset? Do you need someone who will push you? Someone who will ask a lot of questions?

Think about what you specifically need in a mentor, and find who best fits that.

Also keep in mind that any mentor you find may teach you lessons about various aspects of your life. Suppose I'm looking for a financial mentor. When I approach someone who I think would be good, I learn that he's passionate about his wife, family, and friends. I might realize that I want more passion in my life. Just because he's my financial mentor, that doesn't mean I can't learn other lessons from him.

SENSEI AS MENTOR

A martial arts gym is different from a normal gym. In a normal gym, you have access to weights and machines, but nobody's guiding you. When you go into a martial arts gym, you automatically have an instructor to guide you. In a way, your instructor is a mentor. They've walked the line you're trying to walk. When another person walks the path before you, that's called "sensei."

If someone has walked the path before, they can show you how to walk the same path. By learning from their experience, you can become better than who you are. You can also become better than the person who taught you.

ONLINE MENTORSHIP

In today's society, it's easier to find a mentor than it used to be. Now, we have access to the internet. We all have phones. There are countless ways to do research. Chances are there is more than one martial arts school in your area, if that's what you're looking for. Check them out. Which ones seem like the best fit?

Not all mentors, however, will live in your community. But that doesn't have to be a problem. With modern technology, you can easily FaceTime your mentors. You can also email back and forth and speak to them over the phone. Things today are different to how they were years ago. You don't have to travel far to find a mentor anymore.

The one thing you should *always* do, of course, is talk to your parents for help in your search for a mentor. Unfortunately there are people out there willing to take advantage of people with the courage to ask for help, and having an adult's guidance will help make sure you're finding the right person.

LEARN TO LISTEN

Finding a mentor is only the first step. Once you find a mentor, you have to be willing to listen to them.

When a fighter wants to fight, they listen to their coach. If they don't listen to their coach, they won't be able to fight well.

Lessons are easy to learn when you listen to directions. The more you listen, the better you'll become.

When you don't listen to directions, lessons become much harder to learn. When you're doing it all yourself and not listening to your mentor, you're choosing to learn the hard way. Sometimes doing things the hard way is admirable, but if your mentor is showing you the best way, listen. A mentor has already made many mistakes themselves. Any good mentor wants to give you all the tools you need to achieve your goals.

There will be challenges no matter what. Don't add challenges you don't need.

A MENTOR'S STORY

When I was younger, everybody thought I had money because I had a nice car. In reality, I struggled to eat. I never went out because I couldn't afford to. But I wanted to have a nice car so that people thought I was making money.

At that time I had a mentor as a martial artist. Every single day, he would give me one thing. He challenged me to teach martial arts to kids. I had no choice to be away from the limelight. Teach, be responsible, and learn to open my own martial arts school later.

My goal was simple, but not easy: save the money and open a martial arts studio.

I knew that if I went out and spent my money, I would

never open a school. That meant I had to make some sacrifices. No partying. No girls. No screwing around.

My friends teased me all the time. "You don't have a girl-friend!" they'd say. "You're no fun! You're boring! Why are you saving money?"

My dad taught me that to reach my goal I had to save, and that was what I did. My dad was one of my most influential mentors and by following his guidance and sticking to it, I accomplished my goal—my dream—of owning a dojo.

BEYOND THE DOJO

A coach is a mentor. So is a sensei. A manager at work might be a mentor. A parent or uncle might be a mentor. A tutor is a mentor.

In my life, I have a couple of financial mentors—a CPA and someone else who helps me grow my business. My martial arts teacher is my mentor in physical fitness as well as spirituality. My nutritionist is my mentor for my diet. One of the biggest mentors in my life is my wife, who has helped me become a better husband, father, and man.

Know what you're looking for, and what you need. You might not necessarily have to go to someone and say, "I need a mentor," but maybe you can say you need a coach or a tutor. Always remember there are lots of mentors in the world.

FOR THE PARENTS

Whether you've thought about it this way or not, here's the truth: you're a mentor.

As a parent you have the toughest kind of mentor's job, because you're on the job at the toughest times. A baseball coach can mentor during practice and games, but when he goes home (if he doesn't have kids), he's off the hook. The baseball team doesn't see him there. Maybe he sets a good example at practice, but sits down with a six-pack of beer in front of the TV as soon as he gets home.

When you get home, even if you want to relax, you're still mentoring, because what you do sets an example for your kids. If the baseball coach's wind-down time isn't the kind of example you want to set for your kids, you have to decide what kind of example you do want to set.

That can be tough. It can be intimidating.

Let me offer a suggestion: The Five Fs.

In my life, I have five Fs to focus on:

- Fate
- Family
- Fitness
- Financial
- Fun

I look for these five Fs every single day. I think about my fate. Did I pray? Did I practice gratitude?

In terms of family, did I kiss my wife? Did I do what I need to be a husband and father?

Every day, I ask myself what I'm doing for my health. Am I working out? Am I staying active?

In a financial sense, I think about what I need to work on. Do I want to be able to have extra money to take care of my kids? Do I want to go on a family vacation?

Ultimately, I want to have fun every single day. At the end of every day I ask myself: Did I have fun today? Did I have fun talking to my wife? Did I have fun going to church? Whatever happens throughout my day, I want fun to be involved.

If you're not sure where to start, start with the Five Fs. If those are your driving forces, setting a good example will likely take care of itself.

CONCLUSION

As humans, we all share this planet. We are one big community. We are individuals, but we are also one. That's why we should love each other. If someone else falls down, you have to decide what kind of person you are. Are you someone who simply looks down at them and goes on your way, or are you someone who helps that person back up?

As we reach the end of this book, I hope you are more inclined to be the person who wants to pick that person up. Often it feels like the world has more hate than love. So much bullying happens in school and on the playground. But you don't need to succumb to that negativity. As a martial artist, you are someone who understands that the lessons you learn inside the dojo aren't meant to stay in the dojo. What would be the point? As a martial artist, your duty is to take your lessons into the world and into your life, and brighten the world around you.

As I prepare to sign off, here are a few final thoughts that I hope you take with you.

GRATITUDE

Every morning when I wake up, the first thing I feel is gratitude. I'm grateful to be alive. I'm grateful to be a dad and to have kids who want to play with me.

Not only am I grateful to be alive, but I'm grateful for another opportunity to be a better version of myself. Every day, I work on being a better parent and mentor. I know how many people look up to me, so I have to keep myself in check. I can't just be good or great. I have to be better. I have to know and recognize my benchmarks.

I have to be awesome. And I'm grateful for the opportunities I have every day to prove that I am awesome to those who count on me.

Being grateful can be difficult at times. It's not something you just automatically feel all the time. Like anything else, you have to practice it. Take the time, right now, to think of the good things in your life. Think of all the things you take for granted and be grateful for them instead. Think of the challenges and struggles you've faced that you might complain about. Now be grateful for those, too. They're helping you become stronger.

Say, for example, I spar with you and you hit me in the head. I could get mad and hit you back harder. But what would I be teaching myself in this situation? Anger.

Now, what if, instead, I am grateful you hit me?

Wait, what?

How could anyone be grateful for being hit?

Like many of the lessons in martial arts, what appears backwards is indeed correct. I'm grateful because now I know my technique needs work. It needed work before we sparred. It needed work yesterday. But I didn't know it until you gave me that gift of a punch to the head. Now I can become better.

CONTROL

In martial arts, your hand is a weapon. Again, what seems backwards is true. Contrary to popular belief, you don't use a weapon to hurt anybody else. You use the weapon to practice controlling yourself.

You may remember the story I told in the chapter on sparring about the young man who yelled outside after being punched. This is someone who was not in control of himself. He stopped training because in order to train, he had to keep control. Wherever he is now, I hope he's learned this lesson. Unfortunately, I doubt he has. Why? Because the dojo is one of the best places to learn control.

Remember that in a dojo you are not just learning to fight. You're learning to be the best you.

HONESTY

Remember, if you can't be honest with yourself, you can't expect anybody else to be honest with you. The first step to having a healthy body is a healthy mind. A healthy mind is an honest mind.

Sometimes people find this hard to hear. The more you're in denial, the more the truth hurts. If you cheat on yourself, you can't expect that nobody will cheat on you. We all have a tendency to blame others. The harsh reality is that sometimes you should blame yourself.

Personally, I don't know anyone in my life who wants less. But if you want more, you have to see where you are first. Find true friends who aren't afraid to give you honest feedback about this and help you embark on your journey toward achieving your goals.

SHARE WHAT YOU'VE LEARNED

In my opinion, you can't call yourself successful if you don't share what you know. If I keep everything to myself, I can't look back at my life and feel proud.

I am thrilled whenever my students beat me. As a teacher, it's my responsibility to teach. That means I have to be willing to share everything I know so that my students can be better than I.

If I'm worried about someone being better than I am, I have to work harder on myself. That's not a positive quality for a teacher to have. If you want to be a true martial artist, then you are a teacher. You are a leader.

KEEP GROWING

Bruce Lee once said, "Empty your cup so that it may be filled."

I love this quote. When you go somewhere, you have to empty your cup. If you choose to learn, you have to be willing to learn. You have to let go of what you know, or what you think you know, to gain new knowledge.

What stops people from learning is fear. Often, they are afraid of being wrong. They're afraid of failure.

They're afraid of being judged. They're afraid to achieve greatness.

Let go of such fears. Embrace the struggles. Find the courage to empty your cup and allow it to be filled, over and over.

THERE'S ALWAYS ROOM TO GROW

These days, people are willing to improve their cars and houses, but they're not willing to improve themselves.

Every single person has room to grow. You can grow as a parent or as a husband or wife. You can grow financially. You can grow in all areas of your life. Remind yourself of this fact every day.

A man who trains at my gym is half-blind, and yet he still does kickboxing. He can still kick and punch the bag. Why? Because he's determined. He made a commitment to grow.

MAKE IT A GREAT DAY

At some point in your life, I'm sure someone has told you to have a great day. People say it all the time. It's a phrase that has all but lost its meaning.

I think it's something we need to say to ourselves more often.

It's your choice if you have a great day or not. You can make any day great, if you choose to.

Bad days happen. But if you want to make your day better, you can. If you want your hair to look better, you can comb it differently or style it with gel. And yet we don't think we can change how we feel. Just like you can change your hair, you can change your attitude. You can make any day greater.

YOUR TURN

When you finish reading this book, look at yourself. Where are you at this moment? Where do you want to go?

This book has given you a lot of information, but if there's one thing I hope you've learned, it's that the entire world is the dojo. When you step out into the world, you step onto to the mat.

Every day, when you wake up, you approach the mat.

Start the day right: bow.

ACKNOWLEDGMENTS

Thank you to Master Hung Nguyen, Master Rocky DiRico, Master Thohsaphon Sitiwatjana, Master Hung Tran, and Tom Cerino for impacting my life and inspiring me to be a better and greater version of myself. Thank you to my parents Cao D. Nguyen and Lap T. Nguyen. A very special thank you goes to my wife, Anna Nguyen for seeing me as bigger than I am. Anna, you are my best friend. I will love you always.

ABOUT THE
AUTHOR

NINJA NGUYEN is the owner of Xtreme Ninja Martial Arts in Medford, Massachusetts. A lifelong martial artist, Nguyen began his training in a small Vietnamese village at four years old, before immigrating to the United States as a refugee with his family during the war in Vietnam. When he's not teaching in his dojo, Nguyen continues his own training under the instructor he has had for the last thirty years. He lives outside Boston with his wife and three children.

57312528R00132

Made in the USA
Middletown, DE
29 July 2019